No Matter What

What

REFLECTIONS for teens

you can rejoice

Books by Michelle Grover

No Matter What: You Can Rejoice

The Girl in the Mirror

michelle grover

No Matter What

REFLECTIONS for teens

you can rejoice

JOURNEYFORTH

Greenville, South Carolina

Cover Photo: Paul Taylor/The Image Bank/Getty Images

Design by Rita Golden
Page Layout by Kelley Moore

© 2008 BJU Press
Greenville, SC 29614
JourneyForth Books is a division of BJU Press

Printed in the United States of America
All rights reserved

ISBN 978-1-59166-820-6

15   14   13   12   11   10   9   8   7   6   5   4   3   2   1

Dedicated
to my absolutely wonderful parents,
Mark & Susan Gons.

Thank you for introducing me as a little girl
to our great God and for
showing me what it means to have
a personal relationship with Him!
I love you!

 and

to my faithful husband, my best friend forever,
Alan Grover, Jr.

You keep me going, love. Thank you for
continually encouraging me to give
everything I have to serve our great God
and for challenging me to always strive
to be beautiful in His sight. You're definitely
"my favorite." I love you!

Contents

Introduction

Have you ever felt like your whole world has been picked up by a monsoon, jumbled around, and then dropped on a deserted island? Where do you turn when you're faced with a muddle of questions and emotions?

I turn to the Psalms. No matter what emotion we're feeling or what mixed-up crises we are facing, we can be fairly confident that one of the psalms expresses our thoughts and reactions pretty well.

During a particularly challenging time in my own life, the Lord kept bringing me back to Psalm 104:27–28. As I started studying the psalm as a whole, the Lord began to show me how He is my great God. My heart was so encouraged. And even though the details of my situation had not changed, I learned that I could praise my great God no matter what!

It is my prayer that as you study through Psalm 104, you will see your great God for Who He really is and that you too will learn to praise Him no matter what.

Please do not feel pressured to do an entire lesson in one day. It is much more important that you really grasp and apply each truth you discover. Our great God is also our Gentle Shepherd who desires to lead us at a pace that we are "able to endure" (Genesis 33:13–14; Psalm 23; Isaiah 40:11).

I trust *No Matter What* will give you the hope and encouragement that you are looking for to keep going in your life and to keep growing in your relationship with Him.

With love,

michelle l grover

Lesson One
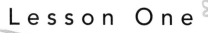
Blessing Our Great God

Opener

I still remember my high school history teacher mimicking—no, it was more like mocking—me as I walked down the hall to his classroom talking to myself—yes, with my hands—trying one more time to get the battles of World Wars I and II straight in my head before the test.

Have you ever had something like that happen to you? Maybe you were in a store or sitting in your car at a stoplight, talking or singing to yourself. How did you feel when you realized someone was watching you, maybe even making fun of you?

Getting caught talking to yourself can be kind of embarrassing. But it doesn't have to be.

As Psalm 104 opens, the psalmist is—you guessed it—talking to himself. Weird? Not really. Because he's telling himself how to think about God and whatever it was that God had allowed or placed in his life. That's not weird. And it's nothing to be embarrassed about either. In fact, it's a very important part of every Christian's life, as you'll discover in this first lesson.

Focus Passage

Read all of Psalm 104, to get the big picture. You may decide you want to do this with each lesson, but our actual focus for this lesson will be just that first phrase in verse 1.

Finding Out God's Greatness

Psalm 104 begins and ends—apart from a final "hallelujah!" or "Praise ye the Lord!"—with the same phrase. What is that phrase (verses 1 and 35)?

_____

The psalmist does not address himself by name, but rather speaks to which part of himself (verse 1)?

_____

We'll come back to what it means to "bless the Lord," but first let's make sure we understand the "O my soul" part. The soul is that innermost part of your being. Often in Scripture *soul* refers to your heart and/or your mind, which are the centers of your emotions and thoughts.

As girls, we're plenty used to the struggle of keeping our hearts and minds in control rather than having them control us. But God doesn't put in any exception clauses for females in Proverbs 4:23. Look up Proverbs 4:23 and write it below.

_____

_____

_____

_____

_____

The word *keep* could be translated *guard*, and the *issues of life* can be everything about you, including your attitudes, your words, and your actions.

Being a guard is definitely not an easy assignment. Have you ever watched—or teased—one of those men standing outside a citadel or palace, decked out in a fancy uniform with a rifle? Those soldiers are not allowed to say a word or to even crack a smile while they're on duty. Now that takes a lot of concentrated effort.

Do you think that guarding your heart could be any easier? I don't. Those soldiers are guarding a royal palace, but as a Christian, you are guarding the throne room of God—your heart. That's something to take seriously! Remember how Proverbs 4:23 put it: "with all diligence!"

Look back at Psalm 104.

Do we know what this psalmist is going through in his personal life?

_____

Do we even know who this psalmist is?

_____

Some suggest the writer to be David because we know he wrote Psalm 103, and both Psalms 103 and 104 start the same way—"Bless the Lord, O my soul." Many of the verses point back to the truths that God taught Job at the end of that book of the Bible, so perhaps the writer was Job. But we don't really know for sure. We do know that this psalmist was a real person, just like us; and that he had a real relationship with our great God, like you and I must.

One thing that becomes apparent if you compare the individual truths in this psalm with earlier portions of Scripture is that a good number of these truths were previously revealed or taught in other passages, like Genesis, Job, and other Psalms. What that tells me is that whoever wrote this psalm was meditating on the truths he was learning and had learned from the Word of God. As he thought on those truths, he encouraged his heart and began praising his God with this beautiful song!

Do you know the best way to guard your heart? It is to meditate on the truths of God like this psalmist did. You will find God's truths in

His Word, the Bible. As you meditate on the Word of God, you will find His truths protecting and guarding your heart like armor against the attacks of the world, the flesh, and the devil.

If your heart is right with God, diligently guarded against sin and meditating on the truths of Scripture, you will be able to respond correctly to whatever He places into your life, however hard it may be, and to praise the Lord from the depths of your heart.

Okay, we said that your soul is made up of your *heart* and your *mind.* Proverbs 4:23 addressed your responsibility to guard your *heart,* or your feelings and emotions, "with all diligence." But what about the other part of your soul—your *mind* or thoughts? Does God expect you to take responsibility for that too? Are you supposed to be in control of your thoughts?

Read 1 Peter 1:13.

Fill in the blanks:

"Wherefore _____ ____ the loins of your _____" (1 Peter 1:13*a*).

Guess what? Another military illustration. The soldiers in Peter's day wore something like a skirt. They would tuck the long ends of that skirt into their belt so they could run faster and fight harder without tripping and falling. In 1 Peter 1:13, God tells us that He expects us not to let our minds run loose, but to tuck in the loose edges so we can run and fight well in our battle against sin and Satan.

Can you think of some thought that might need *girding up* in your mind? (Helpful Hint: 2 Corinthians 10:5.)

_____

So how *are* you supposed to think? Paul in his letter to the Christians at Philippi gets very specific about the types of things that are good and right for Christians to think about. Read Philippians 4:8. What things are you supposed to think on?

_____

_____

_____

_____

_____

_____

_____

We could launch into another whole study based on that verse, but for now let me just say that Philippians 4:8 can be a very practical and helpful sort of checklist to determine whether the things you are thinking about during the day are things that God would want you to think about. Usually the hardest part is admitting when something that you like to think about doesn't fit into those categories and you have to ask God to forgive you and then start thinking about something else that does fit God's pattern for right thinking.

Back in Psalm 104:1, what does the psalmist tell his soul to do?

"_____ the _____, O my soul."

Again, we don't know who this psalmist is or what he has been going through, but we do know that he told himself how to respond to the God Who orchestrated each event in his life—by blessing the Lord. And that is exactly the response each of us must have regardless of the circumstances in our lives: we must bless the Lord!

But, *"Bless* the Lord?" What does *that* mean? Basically it's just another way of saying, "Praise the Lord!" or "Thank You, Lord!"

Looking at another passage where this same expression is used may help to clarify things. Turn back one chapter in your Bible. How does Psalm 103 begin?

_____

David goes on to tell us two practical ways that we can do that (Psalm 103:1–2).

Fill in the blanks.

1. In Psalm 103:1, it's a matter of blessing His holy _____ and *praising* God for Who He is.

2. In Psalm 103:2, it's a matter of *not* _____ the blessings He gives to us, but rather remembering and *thanking* Him for what He does.

We, too, can bless—praise or thank—the Lord because of His name and Who He is (Psalm 103:1). Look up the following references and discover the name for God. Record how you could bless the Lord because of each of His names.

Blessing God For Who He Is

Verses	Name of God	Blessing That Name
Genesis 1:1; Psalm 139:14 Creation	Elohim: The Creator	I can praise God for making everything including me.
Genesis 16:13 Hagar at her lowest point	El Roi: The God Who Sees	
Genesis 22:6–17 Abraham at the altar with the son who meant the world to him	Jehovah-jireh: The Lord Will Provide	
Exodus 3:3–15 Moses at the burning bush	Jehovah (LORD; Yahweh): The Eternal, Self-Existent One; I AM	

Psalm 23:1 In the Shepherd's care	Jehovah-raah: The LORD my Shepherd	
Isaiah 9:6 The promise of the Messiah	Wonderful Counselor	No matter what my question or problem, I can go to God confident that He will have the answer!
Isaiah 9:6 The promise of the Messiah	Mighty God	
Isaiah 9:6 The promise of the Messiah	Everlasting Father	
Isaiah 9:6 The promise of the Messiah	Prince of Peace	

There is so much to praise God for in the very names He has chosen for Himself.

We can and should also bless the Lord by remembering the good things He has done for us. Read Psalm 103:3–5 and record the *benefits* that David did not forget!

Blessing God For What He's Done
"Forgiveth all thine iniquities"—God's salvation provided for me by Jesus Christ's death on the cross for my sin!

There is *always* something we can be thankful for. In fact, Paul tells us that we must be thankful. Read 1 Thessalonians 5:16–18, and notice that Paul writes these verses as commands, not options.

How often or how long or when should we rejoice (1 Thessalonians 5:16)?

_____

And in what circumstances should we give thanks (1 Thessalonians 5:18)?

_____

Let's get very practical as we close this lesson. There are so many specific ways you can bless the Lord. Here are a few basic ones. I would encourage you to look up the examples for each of these.

1. **In prayer**: *Praise* Him for Who He is—your Savior, your Comforter, your Strength; *thank* Him for what He has done for you—saving your soul from hell and giving you so many other daily blessings.

   Example: Psalm 68:9–10. What was David thanking God for?

   _____

2. **In song**: If you don't already have one, I would strongly recommend your getting a hymnal or a good song book that you keep with your quiet time materials. You will usually be able to find a song that reflects exactly what you would like to say. It's such a wonderful tool to use for memorizing "psalms, hymns, and spiritual songs" (Ephesians 5:19) that you can sing in your heart, or right out loud, throughout your day.

   Example: Exodus 15:1. Who was singing this song? Why (see Exodus 14:30–31)?

   _____

3. **In testimony**: How often are you given opportunities at school or at church or maybe even around the dinner table to share something that God is teaching you? As you talk about our great God with others, you are blessing Him!

   Have you ever noticed how much easier it is to be the second person to share a testimony? As you decide to go ahead and share what God is doing in your life, it makes it easier for your friends to share what He is doing in their lives too.

   Example: Psalm 66:16. Who does this psalmist invite to hear his testimony?

   _____

4. **Just in how you live**: Everyday choices to love others show those around you Who your God is. Your life gives them a very specific opinion about Him. As you live in a way that would please God, you are not only praising Him with your life, but you are giving others reason to praise Him.

   Example: 1 Corinthians 10:31. When are we to glorify God (give others the right opinion of Him)?

   _____

Reflections

When something goes wrong in your life, is your initial reaction to complain, to say you don't care anyway, or to convince yourself to praise the Lord no matter what?

_____

Are you guarding your heart with all diligence?

_____

What enemies do you have to guard against?

_____

What could you do differently to better guard your heart?

_____

What do you think about the most during a typical day? What areas of thinking could you do better in? What area is frequently a challenge for you?

_____

Memorizing Scripture would be a good way to guard your thoughts. What else might help you think the right thoughts?

_____

Pick one of the names of God that means a lot to you. Which one is it? Why?

_____

Is it possible to bless or praise and thank God in every situation in your life?

_____

Is there something challenging that you are going through right now? What is it? And how can you bless the Lord even in the midst of it?

_____

Will you choose to give God praise for being in control of your life?

_____

Will you choose to be thankful in everything?

_____

Write out some specific ways you can bless the Lord today:

1. In prayer: What can you thank Him for today? Or which one of His names are you grateful for?

   _____

2. In song: Can you think of a song you could sing throughout this day?

   _____

3. In testimony: Who could you share with about what God is teaching you?

   _____

4. In how you live: How could you be a blessing to someone else and give them a right opinion of Who He is?

   _____

Additional Study

Read James 3:9–12. In this passage on the tongue or speech, James points out how we should be consistent in our speech. If we are blessing God with our lips, how should we be treating other people?

_____

How do you treat other people?

_____

What about behind their backs or when they're not around?

_____

Would that please God?

_____

Memory Verse

Psalm 103:1–2

"Bless the Lord, O my soul: and all that is within me, bless His holy name. Bless the Lord, O my soul, and forget not all His benefits."

Lesson Two
Approaching Our Great God

Opener

I don't know how many times I practiced my approach for hitting in volleyball. Our coach had a very specific way she trained us to prepare for that ball. "Toe, toe, heel, heel, spike!" she would shout. But those steps were really only part of the approach. There was the direction of your body, the pullback and swing of your arm, the follow-through, and so on. We practiced that approach in slow motion, in sync as a team, and who knows how many other ways. Can you relate?

The approach you take when hitting a volleyball is important, but so much more important is your approach when you come before our great God. In this next section of Psalm 104:1, we'll see the psalmist's approach to God.

Focus Passage

Read Psalm 104:1*b* (the middle portion of this first verse). Again, you may want to read the whole chapter.

Finding Out God's Greatness

Notice how the writer or singer of Psalm 104 turns from talking to his soul to talking to his God. How does this psalmist approach God (Psalm 104:1*b*)?

"___ _____ _____ _____, Thou art very great!"

We looked at some of the names of God in our first lesson. Without getting into too much detail, let's just note that in Scripture whenever *Lord* is in upper case letters—LORD— it is referring to *Jehovah God*, that is YHWH or Yahweh. This is the name God used when He committed Himself to being our God. You could say it's His "relationship name." Additionally, it is, perhaps, His highest title. And it is with this exalted, yet very personal, name that our psalmist approaches God.

It is so important that as we approach our great God we do so with incredible respect for Who He really is. It's pretty awesome to realize that the God of everything desires a personal relationship with you and me as individuals!

Fill in the blank from Psalm 104:1*b*

"O Lord ____ God . . ."

Not only should we approach God with incredible respect as the psalmist does by calling Him Lord, but we must also approach Him within a personal relationship owning Him as *my* God.

Read 1 Kings 3:16–28. In this dramatic but true-life story, both women exclaimed, "It's *my* baby!" And yet, obviously, only one of them could be his true mother. This drama illustrates that a *claim* to owning something does not necessarily equal true ownership.

On a more serious level, many people today *claim* that God is their God: millions say that they are Christians, yet many of these people do not have a *true* relationship with Him.

In Matthew 7:22–23, what horrifying words does Christ tell people who claim His name and yet do not have a personal relationship with Him?

_____

In my opinion, that is one of the scariest—and saddest—passages in all of Scripture. How many people will have deceived themselves by doing good things in the name of God and not really know Him? How many will claim to be Christians and ultimately find their place in the lake of fire for all eternity?

And yet, God is so good in that He has offered us salvation. If you have accepted Christ's free gift of salvation, you can be confident that you have a personal relationship with Him. Relationships take time and communication to develop. We can praise the Lord that He talks to us through His Word and we can talk to Him through prayer.

As you spend time reading the Bible and praying, you will be amazed at how real God becomes to you and at how much you will be growing in your relationship with Him!

God wants to be your _best_ Friend! If you miss your time with Him, ask His forgiveness and make more determined plans for the next possible time you can spend alone with Him. That quiet time is as important to God as it is to you. He loves you, and He longs to spend time with just you!

In Psalm 104:1*b*, how does the psalmist describe God?

_____

This psalmist is not just reciting a learned line of poetry like the little kid who prays, "God is great. God is good. And I thank Him for my food. Amen." No, he is expressing the unique greatness of God out of a sincere heart conviction. In other words, he really means it and believes that his God is very great! Do you really believe that _your_ God is very great?

_____

There are several ways that we as Christians should respond as we realize how very great our God truly is and how great the things are that He has done for us. Look up the following verses and fill in the ways that we should rightly respond to our God's greatness. Then spend some time considering whether you personally respond these ways to the greatness of our God.

Verses	Ways to Respond
1 Samuel 12:24	"Only _____ the Lord and _____ Him in truth with all your heart..."
Nehemiah 4:14; Psalm 106:21	Remember the Lord; don't forget Him like the children of Israel did. Don't be afraid to fight for what's right.
Nehemiah 8:6; Psalm 48:1	
Daniel 9:4 (Hold your place here, because we'll be coming back to this verse.)	
Titus 2:13 (Notice in this verse that Jesus Christ is "our great God" as well as our Savior.)	

Let's look a little closer at that fourth verse from Daniel 9. Read Daniel 9:4–7. When we see God's greatness, we realize how awful sin really is. Remember how Isaiah responded to seeing the holiness of the Lord? He said, "Woe is me!" (Isaiah 6:5).

Notice the following among the sins of the people in Daniel's day.

- rebellion (Daniel 9:5)

- failure to listen to and/or obey God's proclaimed Word (Daniel 9:6)

- general unfaithfulness and transgression (Daniel 9:7)

Those are some of the same issues that we face in our world today! Can you give any additional or more specific examples of these issues in today's teen culture?

- Rebellion:
  rolling eyes at a parent
  mocking behind a teacher's back

  _____

- Failure to listen to and/or obey God's proclaimed Word:
  in church services or Christian school chapel
  going forward at camp just to get your youth pastor off your back

  _____

- General unfaithfulness and transgression: *To transgress* is to cross the line. God has set up some very specific lines, and His lines do not move. We can't budge them, yet we so often try to. Which of God's principle lines are tempting to push?
  the clothes you want to wear
  music
  physical relationships with a guy

  _____

Now look at Daniel 9:7–8. Against Whom is all sin committed?

_____

Joseph understood this truth as a teenager. When Potiphar's wife attempted to seduce Joseph into an immoral relationship, he responded with horror: "How . . . can I do this great wickedness, and sin against God?" (Genesis 39:9).

And yet so often we forget this truth—or choose to ignore it—and we convince ourselves that it's not really a big deal.

All the while God sees our hearts; He knows our sin; and He waits for us to come to Him like Daniel did with a humble, repentant heart, confessing our sins and asking for forgiveness. Though we have rebelled against Him, He is a God of great mercy and forgiveness (Daniel 9:9). Over and over again, He shows Himself to be so by forgiving you and me and continuing to love us with His never ceasing mercy (1 John 1:9).

Can you think of a time when you have asked God to forgive you for some specific sin and after praying you felt like a weight had been lifted from your heart?

_____

That's what I mean!

Jeremiah tells us that if it were not for God's willingness to forgive and to show us new mercies every morning, we would be utterly destroyed (Lamentations 3:22–23).

But praise the Lord, His mercies *are* "new every morning: great is thy faithfulness" (Lamentations 3:23).

Write out Psalm 86:5 below.

_____

_____

_____

_____

_____

_____

_____

Read over that verse three or four times and let the truth sink in.

As you approach God, know that you have a personal and very special relationship with Him. Then go with an attitude of awe for how very great He is, an attitude of thankfulness for "how great things He hath done for you" (1 Samuel 12:24), an attitude of *humility* confessing your own sin, and an attitude of *praise* for His great forgiveness and everlasting love.

Reflections

Do you approach God with respect when you pray? How about when you go to church to worship Him? Is your attitude one of respect in the services? In youth group?

_____

_____

Take a minute to prayerfully consider your own relationship with the Lord. Can you say in all truthfulness that He is "my God"? And will He say, "You are Mine"?

_____

_____

Are you spending time alone with Him on a daily basis? What could you improve about your quiet time?

_____

_____

Take a minute to consider some of the great things He has done for you (1 Samuel 12:24). Write a few of those things below and then thank Him for each of the things on your list.

_____

_____

_____

_____

_____

_____

_____

As you see God's greatness, do you recognize your own sinfulness? Do you realize that any sin in your life is really against God Himself? Is there any sin in your heart that you need to confess and ask God to forgive you for, right now?

Will you rejoice in our great God's forgiveness?

Additional Study

Do you ever find yourself making excuses for your sin by thinking that God just expects too much from us?

If you would consider what some of the pagan gods supposedly demand from their worshipers, you would realize that the true God really requires very little. Pagan worshipers of false deities are seen throughout Scripture sacrificing their children to the fire (Molech), cutting themselves with knives (Baal), and so on. The people in Micah's day wanted to know what God expected of them. They suggested exorbitant sacrifices. But Micah told them that God had already shown him what He required, that He wanted only what was good. Quite simply, they were "to do justly, and to love mercy, and to walk humbly with [their] God" (Micah 6:8).

Are you doing justly or what is fair and right in God's eyes?

Do you love mercy—withholding punishment or condemnation when someone really deserves a consequence?

Are you walking humbly with God? Or is there pride in your heart?

God is a good God! Because He is righteous, He must punish sin; but because God is love, He is ready to forgive. "Who is a God like thee?" Micah exclaims. Read Micah 7:18 and 19, and rejoice in the unique greatness of our God in His willingness to forgive.

You may also want to look at the following verses that deal with God's forgiveness: Psalm 103:8–14; Isaiah 1:16–20; 38:17; and Jeremiah 31:34.

Memory Verse

Nehemiah 8:6

"And Ezra blessed the Lord, the great God. And all the people answered, Amen, Amen, with lifting up their hands: and they bowed their heads, and worshipped the Lord with their faces to the ground."

Lesson Three

Serving Our Great God as the Great King

Opener

There's something about royalty that intrigues those of us who are not part of that class. Who knows how many books, plays, and screenplays have been written about royal life. You can read everything from the classic novel about a prince who wants out of being royalty to modern movies featuring girls who find out in the midst of their common lives that they really are royalty.

And though it's true that "you shouldn't believe everything you see on TV," doesn't some of it make you wonder what life in the palace is really all about?

Today's lesson takes a look at a King and His royal palace. As Psalm 104 progresses, the psalmist goes from addressing the Lord as his very great God to describing Him as the King of all Creation. So join me, and we'll see up close what royalty is really all about!

Focus Passage

Read Psalm 104:1–4. Our focus will be on the last phrase in verse 1 through verse 4.

Finding Out God's Greatness

Our clothing says a lot about us, starting when our moms first allowed us to pick out our own clothes. Now we won't discuss the preschooler who comes to school in a mismatched array of colors, but as a young woman, your clothing in a sense defines who you are and can even describe how you are feeling before you ever say a word.

Think about it. When you go to your closet in the morning, you take into account the activities of the day. But beyond that, your choice is narrowed by how you feel, or how you want to feel—confident, classic, cool, or just plain comfy—and what your particular preference of color is. "Am I in the mood for pink, lime green, turquoise, or cobalt?" How many times have you actually put something on only to decide that's not really what you wanted to wear?

God's clothing, similarly, says a lot about Him. And because He never changes (Hebrews 13:8), His clothing has no need to change either. You see, His clothing is His character, His divinely unique attributes. What He has robed Himself in suits Him perfectly at all times and for all time.

It is important to remember that this specific passage (Psalm 104:1–4) highlights our great God as King. His wardrobe perfectly suits that exalted position. Keeping Who He is in mind, let's take a look at the specific garments of His royal wardrobe laid out in Psalm 104.

What two things clothe our King in Psalm 104:1c?

The following definitions will help you understand those two articles of clothing a little better.

- Honor: also translated beauty, splendor, majesty, glory, comeliness, or radiant appearance

- Majesty: literally, an ornament; also translated honor, glory or excellency

These two words are so closely related, it is almost as if honor is the robe and majesty is the ornamentation or detailing on that robe. Woven together, *honor* and *majesty* make a garment fit only for our great God and King.

It is interesting that those given the power to rule have traditionally taken one of these two words as a title; even today, judges are typically addressed as *Your Honor*, and kings and queens as *Your Majesty*.

What additional garment does our King wear in Psalm 104:2?

_____

What do we discover in 1 John 1:5?

_____

Truly, He is not only clothed in light; He is Light!

What does Isaiah 2:5 invite us to do?

_____

As you spend time with God, you will experience what it means to walk in His light. His light chases away all the dark spots in our lives. It is in our darkest hours that we must turn to the light of His glorious presence because "in [His] presence is fullness of joy" (Psalm 16:11)!

Throughout Scripture, we find attributes or character qualities referred to as articles of clothing that God intends *us* to put on. Look up the following references to discover a few of these characteristics.

Verses	Characteristics
Ephesians 6:10–18	
1 Peter 3:3, 4	
Proverbs 31:25	

In Romans 13:14, we are instructed to "put ye on the Lord Jesus." Putting on Christ is the continual day-to-day process called sanctification, which is simply a Christian's being changed to be more like Christ. This process of sanctification is accomplished as you and I obey the biblical model for change found in Ephesians 4:22–24—"put off" the old sinful, selfish desires, "renew" your mind with the cleansing water of His Word, and "put on" a completely new life through Jesus Christ.

Next in our passage for today, we see a description of the King's court (Psalm 104:2b–3a). I would like to focus our attention on the curtain. Some translations use the word *tent*.

In oriental history, princes would sit on their thrones inside of an elevated tent—four walls of curtains surrounding them. The psalmist here continues to attribute royalty to our great God. Here he envisions our King sitting on His throne, high above the earth in that great firmament, distinctly set apart from and elevated higher than everything else, and His royal tent curtain is the whole of the heavens.

On a side note, don't be too alarmed if you compare two good translations of Scripture and they use different words, like *curtain* versus *tent*. A little digging into commentaries and other Bible reference tools will usually help you see how two translations that seem different—curtain and tent—can actually fit together quite nicely.

The first phrase in Psalm 104:3 reads, "Who layeth the beams of his chambers in the waters." The waters there are the firmament, which God separated out on the second day of Creation and called Heaven (Genesis 1:6–8). The picture is of our great God building His royal chambers in Heaven.

These pictures of the King's court just reinforce the magnificence of our great God!

Read Isaiah 40:22. Because God is so great as high King over all, what are we humans on earth like in comparison to Him?

We don't often think of ourselves as small insects, but in comparison with how great God is, we really are so small. If we have this humble opinion of ourselves, God can make something significant of our lives (1 Peter 5:6).

After looking at our King's garments and His court, we find out about His modes of transportation. What does He ride as a chariot (Psalm 104:3)?

_____

And where does He walk (Psalm 104:3)?

_____

The most important thing for us to realize with this verse is the omnipresence of our God—He is present wherever we are! When you see the clouds or feel the wind, remind yourself of the awesome presence of our great God. Remember that He is with you no matter where you are.

Finally we see His servants. Look at Psalm 104:4. What two terms are used of those who are serving Him?

_____

What two terms are used to describe their activity?

_____

It is helpful to note that *angels* and *ministers* can be used interchangeably and that *spirits* and *flaming fire* both carry similar ideas of speed and effectiveness.

If you've ever watched footage of a forest fire or seen one in person, you know how rapidly fire consumes anything and everything in its path. As servants of our great God and King, you and I must have firelike motivation. Being "on fire for God" is an awesome thing!

What is the verb that is used in Psalm 104:4?

"Who _____ His angels spirits; His ministers a flaming fire."

So how are these ministers enabled or made able to serve?

_____

As servants of the Lord, it is so important to realize that "it is God which worketh in you both to will and to [actually] do of his good pleasure" (Philippians 2:13). We can do nothing good on our own; all good is accomplished by our great God Who graciously chooses to work through us as His servants.

Psalm 104:4 is quoted in Hebrews 1:7. The context of the book of Hebrews is helpful in understanding the Holy Spirit's emphasis. Throughout the book of Hebrews, the author's purpose is to establish the superiority of Christ over all things first by establishing the superiority of Christ over the angels and then proceeding to show His superiority over Moses, the Levitical priests, the Old Testament sacrificial system, and so on.

Christ is superior to all. "For the Lord most high is terrible; he is a great King over all the earth" (Psalm 47:2).

Read Psalm 103:19–22. Isn't it awesome how that passage and the first four verses of Psalm 104 go together! And our part is the same as we see our great God as the King of everything in both Psalm 103 and Psalm 104: Bless the Lord!

Reflections

Is God King in your life?

_____

Is God's presence real to you? Are you aware of the fact that He is with you all the time? Do you live like He is?

_____

How do you serve the Lord? Do you do it wholeheartedly? Do you do your work "as unto the Lord"? Do you work quickly? Do you accomplish your goals?

_____

Who is it that enables you to serve the Lord?

_____

Will you resolve to serve the Lord and to bless—again, praise and thank—Him with all your heart because of Who He is?

_____

Additional Study

Read and meditate on Psalm 103:19–22 and Psalm 100:2–4. How are we to serve the Lord according to these passages?

_____

One other great thought is that if you have accepted Jesus Christ as your personal Savior, then God is your Father. And since God is the King, you as His child are a princess! Now that's royalty worth getting excited about! So, do you act like a princess of heaven? Just something to think about.

Memory Verse

Psalm 47:2

"For the Lord most high is terrible; he is a great King over all the earth."

Note: _Terrible_ in this verse can mean to be feared, reverenced (_Strong's_) or awesome (NKJV).

Lesson Four

Becoming Beautiful for Our Great God

Opener

Have you ever been discouraged and you know you should read your Bible, but you don't know where to start, so you just start flipping pages looking at verses you've underlined in the past?

Well, that's exactly what I was doing one evening. I came to the Psalms and saw the twenty-second verse of Psalm 55 underlined. "Cast thy burden upon the Lord, and He shall sustain thee: He shall never suffer [allow] the righteous to be moved."

Never moved. The note in my margin identified an alternative translation for the word *moved*: shaken. He won't ever allow the righteous to be shaken. *But I* feel *so shaken*, I thought. *I know I'm not righteous in and of myself, but as a redeemed child of God—a Christian—, He has declared me to be righteous because of Jesus (2 Corinthians 5:21). So why do I feel so shaken?*

Like me, Christians throughout the ages have found themselves in unsettling, *shaky* situations. My husband pointed me to what came before my highlighted verse in Psalm 55 and showed me that David himself was in a very shaky situation (verses 2 and 4–7).

What then was David's secret to feeling *unshaken*? He cast his burdens on the Lord, clinging to His unshakable character, and cleaving to His unshakable Word. That's exactly what I needed—to hand all my worries and problems over to the Lord instead of trying to figure it all out myself.

In this lesson we will find security offered in realizing God's unshakable, immovable foundations for us. We will also explore the blessing of His boundaries.

Focus Passage

Read Psalm 104:5–9 and Job 38:4–11.

Finding Out God's Greatness

Throughout much of the book of Job, both Job and his friends tried to figure out why he was going through the terrible trials that had been placed in his life. Basically, they were trying to figure out God.

Some of his friends determined it must have been some sin in Job's life that caused God to take away his children, his source of income, and his own health. God allowed these friends to speak their minds, but then God Himself spoke to Job with the intent of proving to him that man does not, and cannot, understand the awesome works of God. He used creation as an example.

In Job 38:4–11, God began questioning Job, with the purpose of humbling him. To do this, God pointed out that He didn't have help from man when He created everything. God laid the foundations of the earth, and He therefore has absolute control over it. It's important for us as young women to remember that God also created us and has absolute control of our lives as well. But that's a good thing. I know I wouldn't want to be in control of my own life. I'd mess everything up for sure. It's so much better to trust God. He knows the end from the beginning, and He has the power to make it all turn out right in the end.

As we look at Psalm 104:4, it's important to remember its context—or how this verse fits into the rest of the verses—in the chapter. Who is the *Who* in this verse? (Hint: You may have to trace backwards a little to find the answer.)

Our God, Who is King, is also Creator. Read Isaiah 51:12–16. Take note of the prophet's application of God's power to create.

God alone has the power to create, and He alone also has the power to comfort. Often instead of acknowledging God's greatness, we give in to fearing what other people might think. We forget that those people are as frail as grass that so easily dries up in the hot sun and dies.

We are God's people! And we must rest in the truth that He holds each of us in His powerful yet gentle hand. He's the One that really counts. And He's the One that can offer real comfort and encouragement.

Psalm 104:5 states, "Who laid the foundations of the earth, that it should not be removed [or moved] forever."

The wise king Solomon declared in Ecclesiastes 3:14, "I know that, whatsoever God doeth, it shall be for ever: nothing can be put to it, nor any thing taken from it: and God doeth it, that men should fear before Him."

What does Acts 5:39 tells us about when God does a work?

What does John 10:28 tell us about when God saves?

What does Psalm 104:5 tell us about when God lays the foundations of something?

And what else does Psalm 55:22 tell us God will not allow to be moved (or shaken)?

Read Psalm 55:16–17. What did David do in this difficult time, confident that God would hear and answer?

_____

Now read Psalm 55:18, and discover how David's confidence grew. Even in the midst of a crisis, David experienced what emotion?

"He hath delivered my soul ____ _____ from the battle . . ."

Read Psalm 55:22 and note that ultimately, David was able to use his experience to challenge others to do what he had done—to hand over their problems to the Lord and to claim His stability and security.

As we return to Psalm 104, we pick up with verses 6 and 7. Verse 6 is a statement of what the earth looked like on the first day of creation (Genesis 1:2). Verse 7 tells what happened on the third day of creation (Genesis 1:9). In verse 7, what did it take for the waters to flee and haste away?

_____

And where did they go (Psalm 104:8)?

_____

You can exchange the word *founded* for *established, assigned,* or *set up* if that helps you understand the idea here better. The waters went exactly where God wanted them to go. He created each molecule of H_2O with a very specific assignment, and all those water droplets flowed exactly where He told them to, obeying His commands.

In Psalm 32:8, David shares God's own testimony: "I will instruct thee and teach thee in the way which thou shalt go: I will guide thee with mine eye." Just like you can understand exactly what a parent or a close friend is trying to communicate by just a quick glance of the eye, God wants you to understand what He wants you to do and to do it that quickly.

David goes on in Psalm 32:9 to challenge us, "Be ye not as the horse, or as the [stubborn] mule, which have no understanding: whose mouth must be held in with bit and bridle, lest they come near unto thee." God doesn't want to have to put a horse bridle on you to yank you into obedience. Perhaps you've heard of someone that was in a horrible car accident or lost a loved one, and his or her testimony is, "That's what it took for God to get my attention."

What does it take—or will it take—for you to obey God?

We would all do well to learn a lesson from the water drops: hear God's Word, and obey . . . no matter what He may ask you to do. Just like the water, He has a place that He has established just for you, and that place is where you will be happiest. Sometimes it takes a while to figure out exactly where God wants you, but so often His special place for you is found by simply obeying what you know He has said in His Word. As you read your Bible, be looking for direct commands from the Lord and ask yourself if you are obeying those commands. If you truly love God, you will want to obey His commands, and you will realize that "His commandments are not grievous" (1 John 5:3). In other words, when you really love God, what He tells you to do will not be a burden or a big deal. You will want to obey, because you love Him and because you know He loves you and wants what's best for you!

Not only has God directed where the waters should flow, but He has also set up boundaries for them. Look back at Job 38:8a. What picture does God give for His boundaries on the waters?

What picture does He give in Job 38:10?

And what did He tell the waters in Job 38:11?

God sets boundaries and limitations for us as well. He may not set up rock piles and dirt mounds to block us in as He does for the water in a river, but He often sets up limits for us in other ways. It may be a physical limitation like a diagnosis of MS or diabetes, a house fire that leaves scars and handicaps, or simply a small frame or a weak constitution. It may be a mental limitation, formally diagnosed or otherwise. Or it may be some other difficult situation that God allows into your life that you cannot escape.

By allowing limitations in your life, God has given you the liberty to become beautiful in His sight. But you have to choose to see it that way.

Let's look once again at water as an illustration. Have you ever seen a waterfall pouring over the side of a mountain? Or perhaps you can recall a river winding merrily through the woods? Both are pictures of power and beauty. But waterfalls are shaped by their limitations, and rivers flow amidst boundaries of rock and soil. God orders their paths; He directs their courses; He *limits* their ways. And the result is unquestionably beautiful!

God desires to use the limitations in your life to show His power and majesty as well. He wants your life to be beautiful, and for you to be like that river—not complaining at the pebbles along the riverbed, but moving gracefully and joyfully along, sparkling in His light, progressing along His path to His chosen destination for you.

You might be wondering, "What is His chosen destination? How can I ever become beautiful in His sight?" God's goal for you is Christlikeness. And you become Christlike and beautiful by submitting your heart to the Word of God each day and obeying Him in every area of your life.

Reflections

Do you believe God is in control of your life?

_____

Do you trust Him to give you what is good for you?

_____

What should you do when you are feeling shaken (Psalm 55:22)?

_____

Does God have a specific plan for your life?

_____

What limitations or boundaries has God given you?

_____

Will you choose to see God's limitations as opportunities for you to become beautiful to Him?

_____

Additional Study

In Job 38:11, God told the waters, "[This far] shalt thou come, but no further: and here shall thy proud waves be stayed." Notice the adjective God uses for the waves: proud! If there's anything God will not tolerate, it's pride. God will not allow anything or anyone to puff itself or herself up in pride and be exalted over Him. He is a jealous God. And He has every right to be. There is no one like Him!

Sometimes God sets up limitations in our lives just to shut the pride out and make us humbly dependent on Him. That's exactly what He did for Paul. Read 2 Corinthians 12:7–10. According to verse 7, what was Paul given?

_____

Why was this "thorn in the flesh" given to him (also 2 Corinthians 12:7)?

_____

"Lest I should be exalted above measure" is just another way of saying "just so I wouldn't be puffed up or proud" about what God had done in his life.

In 2 Corinthians 12:8, Paul asked the Lord three times to take this limiting thorn out of his life, but God said that wasn't His plan. Instead, what did God tell Paul was sufficient or enough (2 Corinthians 12:9)?

_____

Grace is God's enabling or strengthening you to accept and to act according to His plan for your life.

Paul accepted God's grace and decided he must then do what (2 Corinthians 12:9–10)?

_____

What two reasons does Paul give for glorying in or taking pleasure in his infirmities (2 Corinthians 12:9*b*, 10*b*)?

_____

_____

There is nothing wrong with asking God to remove a thorn or limitation, but if God's repeated answer is "No, it is My will that you remain as you are," it is vital that you accept His plan for your life as both good and best.

Remember, God loves you! And He will only give you those things that will make you more beautiful to Him and more like His Son, Jesus Christ. Humility is one of those qualities that we see in Christ and that is absolutely beautiful to our great God.

Memory Verse

2 Corinthians 12:9

"And He said unto me, My grace is sufficient for thee: for My strength is made perfect in weakness. Most gladly therefore will I rather glory in my infirmities, that the power of Christ may rest upon me."

Lesson Five

Singing to Our Great God from a Contented Heart

Opener

Imagine Kedra hiking up a mountain. It's hot. She's sweaty. *And* she's already drained her water bottle. She and her friend, Jen, are almost to the top when they spot a little fresh mountain spring! What does Kedra do?

She takes off running for it, of course! Kneeling, Kedra cups her hands and drinks in the cool water. Health-conscious Jen is sure it's not fresh and takes Kedra's picture so she'll have a memory in case she dies from bacteria in the water. Kedra just laughs, splashes her face, and fills up her water bottle for the remainder of the hike. One last handful, and she's ready to go again!

The Bible refers to many refreshing springs. And today our study takes us to a special spring located in a valley—a spring at which we will learn to be satisfied with our great God and to sing His praises.

Focus Passage

Read Psalm 104:10–12.

Finding Out God's Greatness

Can you picture this passage—the springs flowing among the valleys and hills, winding and turning, rippling and glowing? Imagine that you can see as a wild donkey creeps up to the water's edge, stoops its neck, and drinks in refreshment. And then, hearing a happy little whistle, you look up to see birds chirping a song without words.

This passage in Psalm 104 truly paints a beautiful picture for us. But it also has some fabulous truths for us to learn—from springs and sparrows. So let's continue our trek through this psalm.

Who is doing the sending forth (verse 10)?

_____

What is being sent (verse 10)?

_____

Where does He send the springs (verse 10)?

_____

What is the purpose for sending the springs there (verse 11)?

_____

Here we see God providing a spring of fresh water to quench His thirsty animals. I am sure there are plenty of animals that no human eye will ever see. Yet God provides for them. If God provides for every beast, He most certainly will provide for your needs and mine. Consider the following verse:

"But my God shall supply all your need according to his riches in glory by Christ Jesus" (Philippians 4:19).

This verse is so often quoted, but I wonder how often it is truly believed.

Stop and think about that for a moment. Do you believe—really believe—that God will meet every one of your needs?

_____

Sometimes we don't realize what our true *needs* are. In John 4, Jesus, "being wearied with his journey," asks the Samaritan woman for a drink from the well of Jacob. She questions His asking her for water because "the Jews have no dealings with the Samaritans."

Jesus responds by saying that if she knew Who was asking her for water, she would have asked Him for a drink, and He would have given her living water (John 4:10).

Read John 4:5–15. This woman obviously didn't get it. Even down in verse 15, she is still thinking in terms of physical thirst. If you read the rest of the passage, you will see how the Lord brought her and many other Samaritans to realize that the satisfaction that He was offering was in a relationship with Himself, the Messiah.

Read Isaiah 55:1–3. Who is invited to come to the waters for a relationship with Christ?

_____

Truly, "with [God] is the fountain of life" (Psalm 36:9).

Read Psalm 63:1–5. David uses this idea of God being the fountain of living waters. In what kind of land (what type of circumstances) do David's soul and flesh seek the Lord (verse 1)?

_____

What is better than life itself to David (verse 3)?

_____

What is David's response to the Lord (verse 4)?

_____

Was David's thirsty soul (verse 1) satisfied in God (verse 5)?

Only God can satisfy your soul!

In Jeremiah, God is grieved with Judah because they have forsaken Him as their fountain of living waters and have tried to substitute other gods for Him. God refers to these substitutes as "broken cisterns, that can hold no water" (Jeremiah 2:13). Any object or person, event or emotion that any of us try to substitute for God will never satisfy.

Let's look back at Psalm 104. We've been looking at the springs and the beasts, but now let's go on to verse 12. As you turn your eyes from the donkeys drinking by the stream and look up into the trees, what do you see (verse 12)?

What have these birds made by the springs (Psalm 104:12)?

If God is the fountain of living water, then just like these little birds, we Christians will be happiest when we make our nest close to Him. Plants grow great on the banks of a river, and I can just imagine a fat little bush with plenty of ripe berries growing right underneath this bird's nest. In Psalm 84:11, we find that we too will not lack "any good thing" as we live in close fellowship with our great God.

Let's go ahead and look at Psalm 84, because earlier in that psalm, we find some more birds. Read Psalm 84:3. Where have the sparrow and swallow in this verse made their homes?

The psalmist goes on to write, "Blessed are they that dwell in thy [God's] house: they will be still praising thee" (Psalm 84:4).

If only we would be as smart as these little birds and choose to live in the altar of God. The apostle Paul wrote emphatically, "I beseech you therefore, brethren, by the mercies of God, that ye present your bodies a *living sacrifice*, holy, acceptable unto God, which is your reasonable service" (Romans 12:1). It is so important that we give our lives to God, willing for Him to do with us as He pleases. Living surrendered to God—"in the altar"—is the best place to live. It is our "reasonable service," but it is also where we will find our greatest delight and joy!

What do we find the birds in Psalm 104:12*b* doing?

_____

God's design for you and me is for us to live surrendered, joy-filled lives. His desire is that we would be able to respond to whatever He puts in our lives with singing—just like the birds in Psalm 104.

Ecclesiastes 2:26 tells us that "God giveth . . . that is good in his sight." If you and I believe that, then we ought to "Praise the Lord; for the Lord is good: sing praises unto his name; for it is pleasant. . . . For I know that the Lord is great, and that our Lord is above all gods. Whatsoever the Lord pleased, that did he in heaven, and in earth, in the seas, and all deep places" (Psalm 135:3–6).

"Sing unto Him, sing psalms unto Him" (Psalm 105:2).

Write out Psalm 147:1 here, and take just a minute to ask yourself if your heart agrees.

_____

_____

_____

_____

_____

Reflections

Will you trust our great God to supply all of your needs—physical, emotional, social, and spiritual?

_____

Is there anything or anyone that you have tried to substitute for God in an attempt to be satisfied?

_____

Have you accepted God's offer of living water, the salvation from your sin through Jesus Christ's sacrifice?

_____

As a child of God, will you live on the altar, surrendered to Him as a "living sacrifice" (Romans 12:1)? Is there something in your life that you've been clutching instead of giving it to God?

_____

Do you enjoy singing to our great God?

_____

Why should you sing to the Lord? What can motivate your songs?

_____

Additional Study

Singing is a way your heart responds to the Lord. It is an evidence that you are being filled with the Holy Spirit or controlled by Him. Over and over, the psalmists exhort us to "sing unto the Lord!" And throughout Scripture, we see God's people responding with joy to Him by singing.

In Psalm 137, the Israelites, having been taken captive by the Babylonians, were perplexed or confused and troubled at how they could possibly "sing the Lord's song in a strange land" (verse 4).

Paul and Silas, however, were able to sing as prisoners in the jail at Philippi. Read their prison experience in Acts 16:22–34. Why do you think these two men were able to respond in this type of a situation with singing?

_____

What results did their singing have?

How you respond to tough times in your life is a testimony to others as well. No matter what comes your way, you can choose to respond by singing. God is worthy of your praise, and He will enable you to sing!

Memory Verse

Ephesians 5:18b–20

". . . be filled with the Spirit; speaking to yourselves in psalms and hymns and spiritual songs, singing and making melody in your heart to the Lord; giving thanks always for all things unto God and the Father in the name of our Lord Jesus Christ."

Lesson Six

Finding Strength and Satisfaction in Our Great God

Opener

Discontent with her grades, unhappy about her family's level of income, dissatisfied with her looks and abilities, Kara walks through life with a frown on her face and the hat from her most recent pity party sitting on her head. She thinks to herself, *If only I were like Britney, then I'd be happy. Why do some people have all the luck?*

Do you know anyone like Kara? (You don't need to write her name down if you do!) More importantly, are you tempted to think, *If only   (you fill in the blank) , then I'd be happy?*

This lesson's aim is to remind us that God has already given us everything we need to be happy. And rather than mentioning the sunshine, our psalmist starts out talking about—of all things—the rain!

Focus Passage

Read Psalm 104:13–15.

Finding Out God's Greatness

What is being provided for in Psalm 104:13*a*?

The psalms are poetry, and poetry uses unique word pictures to communicate creatively. Here God's chambers refer to rain clouds. What then is God sending down from these chambers (Psalm 104:13a)?

_____

Ezekiel 34:26 uses the phrase "showers of blessing." It is true that God sends destructive rainstorms at times (see Ezekiel 38:22 and Proverbs 28:3), but for the most part, in Scripture, rain is a blessing from the Lord.

Look at Psalm 147:7–9. Rain is given as a reason to do what (verse 7)?

"_____ unto the Lord with _____;

_____ _____ . . . unto our God."

According to Jeremiah 5:24, what is another proper response when we realize that it is God Who is in control of even the rain? (Note: The people Jeremiah was speaking to did *not* have this response.)

"Let us now _____ the _____!"

In Psalm 104:14, what is caused to grow by the rain?

_____

For what purpose does it grow?

_____

Is it obvious to you that God cares for His creatures?

_____

In Job 38, amidst a multitude of rhetorical questions, God points out that He makes it "rain on the earth, where no man is; on the wilderness, wherein there is no man" (verse 26). Who else could sustain these places? No one but God knows or even cares that they exist!

Read carefully Matthew 6:26–34. If God takes care of the birds and the lilies, will He take care of you?

_____

Jesus Christ wants you and me to have faith in God for our daily needs rather than worry about them. We must trust the Lord! How, after all, did Christ describe these people (end of verse 30)?

_____

According to Matthew 6:33, when will "all these things . . . be added unto you"?

_____

As we go back to Psalm 104, we see the remainder of verses 14 and 15 centering on God's providing for man.

What grows "for the service of man" (Psalm 104:14)?

_____

And both the cattle being fed and this vegetation growing are for what purpose (Psalm 104:14b)?

_____

Our human dietary needs are met by God sending the rain and providing means for food. And whether it's a nice, juicy hamburger or a fresh, leafy salad with hard-boiled eggs and bacon, we can rejoice because God gave it to us! What's your favorite meal? Can you think of how God has provided for each of the ingredients that go into that dish?

_____

_____

What else does God give to us in Psalm 104:15? Fill in the chart with what He gives and His purpose for it.

What God Gives	Why God Gives It

Let's look a little deeper into these three gifts from God.

In Bible times, wine was frequently referred to as a blessing from the Lord. The wines sold in today's culture most certainly are stronger than those served in Bible times, but you don't have to feel like you're somehow missing out because you don't drink alcohol. God never intended His people to misuse this gift. Instead, think of all the wonderful beverages we have today that the people in Bible times never got to enjoy—sparkling water, cappuccino, fruit smoothies, to name a few. God loves to give His people special things that will encourage their hearts and make them happy. He delights to give us all kinds of good things. Remember that God intends for us to do everything—including enjoying these kinds of blessings—in moderation. As they say, "Too much of a good thing is not a good thing!"

Can you think of something special that God has given you to enjoy?

_____

The second blessing in verse 15 is "oil to make his face to shine." Oil, again, is a blessing from God and a symbol of joy. It was considered a necessity in eastern cultures due to the hot, dry climate, much like hand moisturizers are for those of us living in regions where the winters are bitter and cold. Anointing one's face with oil was as common as taking a bath. In fact, if someone did not anoint her face with oil on a given day, she would have been thought to be in mourning.

And lastly, God gives us "bread which strengthen[s] man's heart" (verse 15). Carbohydrates or breads provide our bodies with energy and strength. When my brother and sister and I were in high school, my mom faithfully prepared pasta for us the night before a volleyball, soccer, or basketball game to give us that extra edge of energy. When we go without bread, we become physically weary. But by taking in even a small portion of bread, the stomach is satisfied . . . and the heart is encouraged.

These three—bread, oil, and wine—when mentioned together in the Bible are symbolic of all physical blessings.

Let's look at some parallels of these physical blessings with their spiritual counterparts found in Christ. Let me encourage you to look up the passages listed so you can read them for yourself.

Wine Matthew 26:27–29	At the Last Supper, Christ invited His disciples to drink of the "cup" (wine) which is a symbol of His blood. All who come and drink of Christ will be forgiven of their sins. If that doesn't make our hearts glad, nothing will!
Oil Ecclesiastes 8:1; 1 Corinthians 1:30; Daniel 12:3	"The wisdom of a man maketh his face to shine." In the New Testament, Christ is our Wisdom! As we learn of Him, our faces too will shine. And just as oil was used as a daily practice, we must be seeking Wisdom (Christ) daily in His Word!
Bread Matthew 26:26; John 6:35	Again, at the Last Supper Christ spoke of the bread as symbolic of His body. Earlier, He had identified Himself as "the Bread of Life" promising that "he that cometh to me shall never hunger." And we, through Christ, have all the sustaining strength we need!

Just as wine, oil, and bread were given to man as both necessities and blessings, God has given to you and me His Son, Jesus Christ! He is all we could ever need and everything we really want! As David sang in Psalm 23, "[Because] the Lord is my Shepherd, I shall not want [lack any good thing]."

Going back to Psalm 104, take one more look at verse 13. How is the earth referred to in the second half of that verse?

Another word for *satisfied* is *content*. We, like the earth, are provided for by the Lord. Therefore, we too, like the earth, must be "satisfied with the fruit of [God's] works" (Psalm 104:13).

God has given us physical sustenance; but He has also "blessed us with all spiritual blessings . . . in Christ" (Ephesians 1:3). How can we be dissatisfied with that?

As you claim Christ and see the blessings that God has offered to you in Him—"wisdom, and righteousness, and sanctification, and redemption" (1 Corinthians 1:30)—you will find satisfaction.

And as you do, I think you will find yourself able to rejoice no matter what He gives to you each day.

Reflections

Do you respond to the rain with thanksgiving and praise to God (Psalm 147:7–9)? Or are you more likely to complain about it giving you a bad hair day?

Do you respond to God's power over the weather by fearing or reverencing and respecting Him (Jeremiah 5:24)?

Do you trust God to take care of your needs or are you like the people whom Christ addressed as "O ye of little faith" (Matthew 6:30)?

Are you satisfied and content with what God has given you? Have you thanked Him for His kindness to you recently?

Have you claimed Christ as your "wine, oil, and bread"—everything you need to be happy and have a full life?

Take some time to reflect on the truths in the last chart (page 48) about Christ being our "wine, oil, and bread."

Do you believe *you* can be satisfied with Christ alone?

Additional Study

God provided food for His people in the wilderness. Read Numbers 11:4–34. Note that the place "Kib-roth-hat-ta-a-vah" in verse 34 can be literally rendered "Graves of Craving/Lust." How should our attitude differ from the Israelites concerning God's provisions for us?

Memory Verse

Psalm 84:11

"For the Lord God is a Sun and Shield: the Lord will give grace and glory: no good thing will He withhold from them that walk uprightly."

Remember that if God withholds something from us, then either we are not living in a way that pleases Him or it would not be good for us at the time.

Lesson Seven
Accepting Where Our Great God Has Planted Us

Opener

Saul wanted his son Jonathan to become king after him, but the prophet Samuel had anointed David to be king instead. Jonathan had accepted this plan as from the Lord and had befriended David, but King Saul was determined to have David killed.

Now David is on the run! David and his small band of men find themselves in desperate need of nourishment. David goes to Ahimelech, the priest at Nob, and obtains some of the holy bread for himself and his men to eat. But a man named Doeg overhears David's plot and heads back to King Saul.

Doeg, desirous of personal fame and fortune, unveils David's plan to King Saul. Upon hearing of Ahimelech's assistance to David, King Saul orders that *all* the priests of Nob be killed. Saul's guards refuse to kill these priests, choosing to obey God rather than man. However, Doeg does not honor the Lord in this matter and slays eighty-five priests as well as many other persons and animals in Nob.

Abiathar, one of Ahimelech's sons, escapes to David. And, as a result, David's life is preserved (1 Samuel 20–22).

As David thought about the wickedness of Doeg, he penned Psalm 52. "Why boastest thou thyself in mischief, O mighty man? . . . God shall likewise destroy thee for ever, he shall take thee away, and pluck thee out of thy dwelling place, and root thee out of the land of the living. . . . The righteous also shall see, and fear, and shall laugh at him: Lo, this is the man that made not God his strength; but trusted in the abundance of his riches, and strengthened himself in his wickedness" (verses 1 and 5–7).

Rather than ending the psalm with the condemnation of the wicked, David concludes with the blessing of the righteous: "But I am like a green olive tree in the house of God: I trust in the mercy of God for ever and ever. I will praise thee for ever, because thou hast done it: and I will wait on thy name; for it is good before thy saints" (verses 8–9).

In this lesson you will learn about "the trees of the Lord" and discover practical applications for your life so that you, like David, will be able to say, "I am like a green olive tree in the house of God," know what that means, and be able to praise our great God for making you and for putting you right where you are!

Focus Passage

Read Psalm 104:16–18.

Finding Out God's Greatness

Which kind of tree was planted in Lebanon (Psalm 104:16)?

_____

Who planted them there (Psalm 104:16)?

_____

Do birds live in cedar trees (Psalm 104:17)?

_____

In what kind of tree does the stork make her home (Psalm 104:17)?

_____

Psalm 104 has been referred to as the creation Psalm, so let's take a look back at the Genesis account of creation. Read Genesis 1:9–13. Which day were the trees created?

_____

Now read Genesis 1:20–23. Which day were birds created?

_____

We can take comfort in the fact that God prepared a place for these creatures *before* He even created them. In the same way, God had a plan for your life long before you were even conceived.

1. Read Psalm 139:14–16. Did God know all about your *physical* makeup before you were born?

    _____

2. Jeremiah was told by the Lord, "Before I formed thee in the belly I knew thee; and before thou camest forth out of the womb I sancti-fied thee, and I ordained thee a prophet unto the nations" (Jere-miah 1:5). God had set Jeremiah apart and had a special plan for his life even before he was born. Do you think God has a specific *voca-tional* plan—what you will do for a living—for your life as well?

    _____

3. Read Ephesians 1:3–6. What did God choose "that we should be" (verse 4*b*)?

    _____

We spend a lot of time as teens and young adults trying to find *God's will* for our lives. Sometimes what we really need to do is to stop stress-ing out about the possibility of missing this mysterious thing we call God's will and simply do His will by trusting Him and obeying His Word, living a holy life that is set apart to please Him. You and I need to believe that He has a plan for each of us. And because He is our great God, we can know He's not going to try to hide His best from us.

What had God predestinated—literally, seen beforehand or planned ahead of time—for us to be a part of, "according to the good pleasure of his will" (Ephesians 1:5)?

_____

What else has He "made us" (Ephesians 1:6)?

_____

"The beloved" in verse 6 refers to Jesus Christ. It is through His blood that we are forgiven and given this wonderful acceptance by God, this adoption as His very own children.

When did He choose this redemptive plan for us (Ephesians 1:4_a_)?

_____

So has God had a plan for your _spiritual_ life since before you were born?

_____

Just as God had a place for the birds before He ever created them, He has had a plan for you—physically, vocationally, and spiritually—since before you even existed. Wow! Isn't that just like our great God?

You know, God made the trees for the birds to dwell in—strong, tall, and full of security. And He has a specific place for us to dwell in as well. But no matter where our physical home is, God's desire is for our _dwelling place_ to be in Him.

According to Psalm 90:1, when has God been a dwelling place for His people?

_____

And how long has He been God (Psalm 90:2)?

_____

You will find more strength and security in God than in any *tree* you've ever dreamed of! He's always been there for you, "from everlasting," and He always will be, "to everlasting" (Psalm 90:2)!

Let's look again at these trees in Psalm 104:16.

"The trees of the Lord _____ _____ _____ _____."

Full of sap? Could there possibly be anything we could draw from that? Actually, yes!

Look up Psalm 92:12–15. Another way to translate *fat* in verse 14 is full of sap. The idea is one of having all the nourishment that is needed. What kind of person is going to "flourish like the palm tree" and "grow like a cedar" (Psalm 92:12)?

_____

God declared you to be righteous the moment you accepted Jesus Christ as your Savior; but there is also the process of sanctification, which we've already talked about some, whereby we are becoming more and more righteous—more and more like Christ.

Read James 1:19–25, and make a special note that the way we get the spiritual nourishment we need to be a righteous woman is by spending time reading and obeying the Word of God!

Write out Christ's promise in Matthew 5:6 below.

_____

_____

Psalm 92:14 refers to the righteous as fat or full of sap, well-nourished and flourishing. Do you remember in the Opener, I promised you'd find out what it means when David says, "I am like a green olive tree in the house of God" (Psalm 52:8)? Well, the word *green* in Psalm 52:8 is the same word translated *flourishing* in Psalm 92:14. The idea is that of being full of life and productive, as opposed to being dried up and useless.

God wants you to be like a fruitful tree. Since trees bring forth fruit "after their kind," what kind of fruit will the righteous produce (Psalm 92:14)? (Hints: Proverbs 11:30; 15:4; Galatians 5:22–23.)

_____

God wants you to be "fruitful"—flourishing or green. But He also wants you to be "blessed"—happy and truly satisfied.

Read Psalm 1:1–3. The person who is blessed and "like a tree planted by the rivers of water" keeps himself or herself away from the wrong crowd (Psalm 1:1) and finds his or her delight in what (Psalm 1:2)?

_____

How often does this person meditate on God's Word (Psalm 1:2)?

_____

We've looked at several passages about trees along with the lessons God teaches. Let's look at just one more before returning to Psalm 104.

In Jeremiah 17, the Lord contrasts those who trust in man with those who trust in God. He again uses trees to illustrate His point. Read Jeremiah 17:5–8. Fill in the comparison chart below with what you find:

Characteristic	Jeremiah 17:5–6	Jeremiah 17:7–8
Overall description	Cursed	
Where he places his trust		
Relationship with God		"Whose hope the Lord is"
Like what kind of tree and where	Heath (shrub) in the desert	
Will not see . . .		(or fear) when the heat (trials or evil) comes

The one who trusts in the Lord is the one who is happy and blessed, vibrantly green and full of sap. Remember again David's testimony in Psalm 52:8: "I am like a green olive tree in the house of God: I trust in the mercy of God for ever and ever."

The Lord desires to exchange "beauty for ashes, the oil of joy for mourning, the garment of praise for the spirit of heaviness; that [His people] might be called trees of righteousness, the planting of the Lord, that He might be glorified" (Isaiah 61:3). You see, the Lord is glorified as our great God when He takes all the ugliness of sin and suffering in our lives and miraculously transforms them into beautiful, fruitful testimonies of His grace.

In high school I had a poster hanging on my closet door of a lion cub struggling to climb over a fallen tree trunk. The caption was "Be patient. God isn't finished with me yet." That poster made me smile and keep going so many times when I'd get frustrated. It's not just others that need to be patient with our growth process; we ourselves need to be patient as God works on us. It is good for us to remember that as trees take time to grow physically strong and fruitful, so we take time to grow spiritually strong and fruitful. Trust God to "perfect that which concerneth" you (Psalm 138:8), "being confident of this very thing, that he which hath begun a good work in you will perform it until the day of Jesus Christ" (Philippians 1:6). He will keep working that good work out to its completion—your Christlikeness.

We've spent a good deal of time discussing the trees of Psalm 104:16–17. Let's briefly turn our attention to the mountain peaks. Look at Psalm 104:18.

What do the high hills, the rocks, cliffs, and crags provide for the wild goats and the conies or rock badgers?

God has suited these animals perfectly for their habitat, *and* He has suited their habitat perfectly for them. The wild goats are amazingly sure-footed, which is necessary for their dwelling in the high hills; the rock badgers are "little . . . but they are exceeding wise" for they are "but a feeble folk, yet make they their houses in the rocks" (Proverbs 30:24, 26).

God knows exactly how He made you. He did it on purpose! And God has made a place perfectly suited for you. Your physical and emotional make-ups are not by chance. Neither are the circumstances you find yourself in. God has it all planned out. And just like the wild goats and the rock badgers have the perfect place to call their refuge, we have the ultimate place to call our Refuge in our great God Himself. As believers, we can determine with the psalmist to "say of the Lord, He is my refuge and my fortress: my God; in him will I trust" (Psalm 91:2)!

Reflections

Do you believe that God knows everything about you and has a specific purpose for your life?

_____

Do you believe that God has given you everything you need ("fat" or "full of sap") to be fruitful ("green" or productive) for Him (Psalm 92:14)?

_____

Do you spend time in God's Word on a daily basis (Psalm 1:1–3)? And do you do your best to apply and obey what you read (James 1:21–25)?

_____

Will you determine to place your trust in the Lord and make Him your hope (Jeremiah 17:7)?

_____

Will you determine to not fear or even see when "the heat" comes (Jeremiah 17:8) because your eyes are on the Lord?

_____

Explain Psalm 52:8 in your own words.

_____

_____

Will you claim God as your refuge (Psalm 91:2)?

_____

Additional Study

Read Psalm 37 and Proverbs 2:21–22. Notice the references to dwelling in the land versus being rooted up out of it as a tree. Take some time to examine your own heart for things that may need to be rooted out of your life so that you can enjoy the place, "the land," God has for you.

Memory Verse

Psalm 52:8–9*a*

"But I am like a green olive tree in the house of God: I trust in the mercy of God for ever and ever. I will praise thee for ever, because thou hast done it . . ."

Lesson Eight

Working Diligently for Our Great God and Walking in His Spirit

Opener

At sixteen months old, my little boy was enamored with lions! Anytime he would see a picture or stuffed animal or anything remotely resembling a lion, he would stick his little hands up with his fingers curved like claws, then open his mouth wide and "roar"—silently. It was so cute. But if he's still acting like a lion at sixteen *years* old, that won't be cute anymore!

In today's lesson we'll be looking at our great God's plan for us and contrasting that to His plan for lions. But first, we'll be looking at His creation of the lights in the sky and His purposes for them.

Focus Passage

Read Psalm 104:19–23.

Finding Out God's Greatness

It was the fourth day of Creation. "And God said, Let there be lights in the firmament of the heaven to divide the day from the night: and let them be for signs, and for seasons, and for days, and years: And let them be for lights in the firmament of the heaven to give light upon the earth: and it was so. And God made two great lights; the greater light to rule the day, and the lesser light to rule the night: He made the stars also. And God set them in the firmament of the heaven to give light upon the earth, and to rule over the day and over the night, and to divide the light from the darkness: and God saw that it was good" (Genesis 1:14–18).

Did God have an intended purpose for creating the sun, moon, and stars?

_____

What were God's purposes for creating these lights (Genesis 1:14–15 and Psalm 104:19–20)?

_____

Our seasons are determined by the location of the sun and the moon in their rotations. Can you imagine what life would be like without this God-appointed order to our lives?

_____

We take the sun and moon for granted, but they are set up in the sky testifying of the fact that there is a God Who is ordering everything in the universe!

Read Psalm 19:1–11. In this psalm, David showcases God's two great witnesses to His glory. What is the first great witness (Psalm 19:1–6)?

_____

What is the second great witness (Psalm 19:7–11)?

_____

Just as the Word of God declares God's works and ways, the whole of Creation, and specifically the heavens and its great lights, declares God's works and wonders.

In Isaiah 45:5–9, God asserts His right to be worshiped as Creator and Sovereign over everything. According to Isaiah 45:7*a*, what does God form and create?

In Isaiah 45:9, whom is woe ascribed against?

Fighting God's purposes for us would be as absurd as a clay pot complaining against the potter for how it was made. The sun and moon follow God's prescribed order for their existence, and so you and I must submit ourselves to His creative purposes, always remembering that "God mean[s] it for good"—no matter what "it" is (Genesis 50:20).

As we return to Psalm 104, we see even deeper into God's cycle of day and night. What happens at night (verses 20–21)?

And what happens when day breaks (verses 22–23)?

And each day that cycle is repeated. The beasts go out at night and rest during the day; man goes to work during the day and sleeps in the evening (as a general rule).

Where do "the young lions . . . seek their meat from" (verse 21)?

And so you and I must also seek our sustenance from God. We can and should do our part, but unless the Lord provides, we will find ourselves empty. You must depend on God to "supply all your need" (Philippians 4:19). Remember from Lesson One that one of God's names is "Jehovah-jireh: The Lord will provide!"

So it's God's place to provide, but man has a part too. What is man's part (Psalm 104:23)?

So another reason God has given us light (verse 19) is so that we can work (verse 23).

In his second letter to the Thessalonians, Paul exhorted, "If any would not work, neither should he eat" (3:10). In that exhortation, Paul's main concern was against laziness and being busybodies.

In another epistle his concern was stealing. "Let him that stole steal no more: but rather let him labour, working with his hands the thing which is good, that he may have to give to him that needeth" (Ephesians 4:28).

Work, therefore, provides for our own needs, but it also gives us the ability to help others in their needs.

Gals, it may be easy to pass the buck and say that it is supposed to be men that provide for their families by working, which is true. But it is also very important that we as young women learn to be hard workers. As a side note, when you get to the point where you are considering whom you might marry, it would be wise to make diligence and a good work ethic qualifications for "your man."

Two biblical examples (if they are not the same person) would be Ruth and the woman in Proverbs 31:10–31.

If you will read through Ruth 2, you will find a young woman eager to work with her hands. You will also find that she was blessed and rewarded for her heart to work *and* that she was able to give to others.

The virtuous woman likewise "worketh willingly with her hands" (Proverbs 31:13), is blessed (verses 28–31), and is able to give to others (verse 20).

As we step back and look at Psalm 104:21–23, we can see that God obviously has specific, yet very different, plans for humans and for lions.

Read Ezekiel 19:1–9. This passage is describing two of Judah's kings (Jehoahaz, 2 Kings 23:32–34; and Jehoiachin, 2 Kings 24:6–15), who both *acted like* lions during their reigns. What phrase is repeated in Ezekiel 19:3 and 6?

Compare that concept of devouring others with Galatians 5:14–15. In what ways do you think the Galatians might have been "biting" and "devouring" each other? (Some hints can be found in Galatians 5:26.)

It seems based on the context that these Galatians were taking Christian liberty out of its proper arena and using it to do whatever they wanted to do, cutting down others who had differing ideas. What should they have been doing instead (Galatians 5:14)?

What is love according to Galatians 5:22?

And how are we instructed to walk in Galatians 5:16, 25?

Going back to those kings in Ezekiel 19, how did the prince in verse 6 become a young lion?

We become like those we hang around. It is so important—especially in your teen years when you're making choices and becoming who you will be for the rest of your life—that you choose your friends wisely!

Write out Proverbs 13:20 below.

Ezekiel 19:4 and 8 both illustrate how these kings who were companions with fools and became lions ended up: they were "taken [trapped] in [the enemy's] pit."

What is the result for those who "bite and devour one another" like lions and follow their fleshly lusts according to Galatians 5:19–21?

_____

That's pretty serious! God wants each one of us to inherit His kingdom, which means we will go to heaven when we die! He gave us His Son for that very purpose (John 3:16).

God has purposes for us while we are living as well. God's good intention for you as a young woman is to fear, or reverence, and respect the Lord and to walk in the Spirit, not fulfilling the lusts or sinful desires of your flesh!

As we consider the lights and the lions, we realize God has a specific purpose for each of His creations including you. He loves you and wants you to follow His good intentions for your life—working diligently with your hands and walking in His Spirit.

Reflections

God has a beautiful plan mapped out for your life, just as He has a perfect path for the sun, moon, and stars to follow. Are you seeking to know God's will for your life and submitted to following and obeying His plan?

_____

Remember, doing God's will is often as simple as obeying His Word.

What are God's two great witnesses in Psalm 19? Give an example from each of these witnesses that teaches you something about our great God.

1. _____

_____

2. _____

_____

Are you willing to follow God's plan even if He doesn't answer all of your questions when, or how, you'd like Him to (Isaiah 44)? Is there something that is holding you back from submitting yourself to God? Are you insisting on understanding everything before you take a step? Will you decide instead to let Him direct your path and to trust Him to choose what is best for you? (See Proverbs 3:5–6.)

Do you diligently do the work God has given you, whether it's a household chore, homework, or an actual job?

Are your friends wise or foolish? Do they want to be like Jesus? Are you better off spiritually when you hang around with certain people? Can you think of someone that would be good for you to spend more time with? Is there anyone that you should spend less time with?

Are you walking in the Spirit, evidencing the fruit of that Spirit (Galatians 5:22–24), or are you following your flesh, biting and devouring others, and practicing sinful habits (Galatians 5:15, 19–21)?

Additional Study

Study the evidences or "fruit" of walking in the Spirit (Galatians 5:22–23 and Ephesians 5:18–21). Ask the Lord to show you whether or not these qualities are evident in your life. Are there any that you know you need to work on a little harder? Ask God to help you. He will!

❏ Love

❏ Joy

❏ Peace

❏ Long-suffering (Patience)

❑ Gentleness

❑ Goodness

❑ Faith(fulness)

❑ Meekness (Humility)

❑ Temperance (Self-control)

❑ Singing and making melody in your heart

❑ Giving thanks always for all things

❑ Submitting yourself to one another

Memory Verse

Psalm 34:9–10

"O fear the Lord, ye His saints: for there is no want to them that fear him. The young lions do lack, and suffer hunger: but they that seek the Lord shall not want any good thing."

Lesson Nine

Rejoicing in the Riches of Our Great God

Opener

Have you ever attempted the art of origami? I remember as a young teen checking out a how-to book from the library and being fascinated by the detail and precision of the folded paper and how it turned out looking like a swan or a frog or a Japanese flower. When fashioned properly, the outcome was beautiful!

God's creation is much like origami. It is full of detail and precision and truly fascinating to study. He has put just the perfect number of *folds* into the *paper* of creation.

"O Lord, how manifold are thy works!" cries our psalmist in today's passage. *Manifold* is the word that gives me the picture of origami and its many folds. It literally carries the idea of *many* and *varied*.

In today's lesson, we will be considering the wisdom and wonder behind our great God's many and varied works.

Focus Passage

Read Psalm 104:24–26.

Finding Out God's Greatness

The psalmist has been describing God's workings in so many of His creations. It's no wonder that at this point in the psalm he exclaims, "O Lord, how manifold are thy works!" This singer is excited about our great God and His marvelous creation.

God truly does have so many and varied wonderful works! Review Psalm 104:5–23 and see how many you can list. Include any mention of a created work even if it is not the focus of the verse.

_____

_____

_____

_____

_____

_____

_____

What attribute of God is highlighted in the second phrase of Psalm 104:24?

_____

Let's look up some other verses that highlight this attribute as well. Write down what each verse tells us about our great God's wisdom in the space provided.

Verses	What it says about God's wisdom
Proverbs 3:19–20	
Daniel 2:19–22	

Verses	What it says about God's wisdom
Isaiah 40:13–14; Romans 11:33–34	No one can teach God anything. He has no need for a counselor because He knows and understands everything!
Psalm 139:1–4; 1 Chronicles 28:9	God knows everything about me! He even understands my _____!
James 1:5; 1 Kings 3:9, 28	

God is all-wise. He knows everything about everything—including you!

He knows when you need wisdom, and He is eager and willing to give you wisdom when you ask Him for it in faith believing that He will answer (James 1:5–6).

Let's go back to Psalm 104 and consider the last part of verse 24: "The earth is full of thy riches." If you are using a different translation, your word for *riches* may be *possessions.* Both words fit and can be used interchangeably.

What is it that God possesses that fills the earth? Look at Psalm 33:5*b* for the answer.

_____

Are you surprised? God's goodness fills the earth! Have we not seen several times already the goodness of our great God in Psalm 104?

_____

Paul was also excited about the rich possessions of God. What attributes did he marvel at in Romans 11:33?

_____

Write out Romans 11:33 here:

_____

We could devote the entirety of our lives to searching out the wise workings of our great God and still have only scratched the surface!

What is "the riches of the glory of this mystery" and "our hope of glory" according to Colossians 1:27?

And as you keep reading, you discover in Colossians 2:3 that "in [Christ] are hid" what?

That word *treasures* goes right along with our word *riches*! And truly all the wealth we could ever want is found in Christ.

As we return to Psalm 104, we discover that not only is God's wisdom inscrutable, that is unknowable or not able to be understood (Psalm 104:24), but His created creatures are innumerable—not able to be counted (Psalm 104:25)!

Apparently, if you were to stand on a mountain or high hill in the biblical region of Palestine, you would be able to look out and see the Mediterranean Sea quite easily (*Barnes' Notes: Notes on the Old Testament: Psalms.*, p. 90). I know as I walk along the river at the local park or hike in the woods, my thoughts are often turned to our Creator. I can quite easily imagine that this psalmist was hiking in the mountainous regions of Palestine.

As he looked up at the clouds, he imagined them to be God's chariot. As he headed into the wooded hills, he took note of the valleys and their springs and of the little birds perched contentedly in their branches overhead; perhaps along the way there was a lookout and he could see the fields of vegetation and the grazing cattle down to his right.

As he climbed higher, he saw a little rock badger scurry to his crag and the little goats happily skipping and playing on the distant peaks.

He paused at each of these scenes to marvel at our great God's creativity and love. And as he reached the top, his heart was full!

It is at this point we find him shouting out, "O Lord, how manifold are thy works! in wisdom hast thou made them all: the earth is full of thy riches" (verse 24).

Now that our psalmist has reached the top, he once again pauses to take in the view. His gaze is drawn downward to "this great and wide sea." And he continues his composition.

He thinks of all the creatures that there must be down in that huge sea, perhaps the many and varied fish and corals, each unique and beautiful!

Then he notices what else out in the sea (Psalm 104:26*a*)?

God has created this sea for His own glory, of course, but He has also made it for our good. Think of all the commerce and trade that must have gone on as a result of relations overseas. There were no airplanes in those days, so if there were to be any resources gained outside of the local market, the seas were probably the quickest way for merchants to get where they were going and what they wanted.

In Proverbs 31:14 the virtuous woman is compared to "the merchants' ships" because of her creative resourcefulness and productivity. Are you like a merchant ship in that way? Are you creatively finding ways to accomplish your goals? Are you taking advantage of the opportunities and resources He has given to you?

God has given you so many things so that you can be successful in your daily life—good teaching, helpful tools, and timesaving inventions. Can you think of some specific blessings the Lord has given you that will help you to be successful in life?

He's also given you everything you need to be successful in your spiritual life—prayer, study helps, books, and His Word, the Bible. Let that Word "dwell in you richly" (Colossians 3:16). Colossians 3:16 is a great verse to memorize and claim for your own life! Take a minute to read it right now.

In Psalm 104:26*b*, what else does the psalmist point out down in that "great and wide sea"?

Leviathan is perhaps the most powerful of all God's creation. He was some sort of sea dragon. God gives an extended description of him in Job 41, but for now let's just note what this psalmist gives as God's plan for leviathan. What has God made this creature to do (Psalm 104:26*b*)?

I think we can see here that it is part of our great God's purpose that we as His creatures should have enjoyment and good pleasures.

Obviously we don't want to be hedonists—people whose one goal in life is their own personal pleasure. Scripture tells us that "he [or she] that loveth pleasure [for pleasure's sake] shall be a poor man" (Proverbs 21:17). But God's Word also tells us that the living God, in Whom we are to trust, has given us "richly all things to enjoy" (1 Timothy 6:17).

Where is it, after all, that we find "fulness of joy" and lasting pleasure (Psalm 16:11)?

As you meditate on this passage, rejoice in our great God's manifold works. Praise Him for giving you the means to be prosperous and to enjoy godly pleasures. And thank Him for His Word.

Reflections

Since God is wise, can you go to Him in His Word with any problem and expect to find the right answer?

_____

Have you seen God answer your prayers for wisdom?

_____

Is God rich enough to take care of all your needs? Will you trust Him to do so?

_____

Are you using the rich resources He has given you so that you can be successful?

_____

What resource(s) has God given you that you would like to make better use of—perhaps money, time, His Word, wise parents, good teachers, or something else?

_____

Do you enjoy the good things God has given you? Or do you find things God has forbidden either in His Word or through your parents to be more pleasurable?

_____

Are you spending time in God's Word as a personal, daily practice and letting His Word "dwell in you richly" on a regular basis (Colossians 3:16)?

_____

Are you rejoicing in our great God today?

Additional Study

Not only are God's works of creation manifold, but the works He does in your life and my life are wonderful as well. Read Psalm 40:5–6. Spend some time thinking about how much God must love you to think about you that much! Can you trust Him to do what is best for you?

You may also want to look into the passages on leviathan. He is mentioned in Job 41, Psalm 74:14, and Isaiah 27:1. One specific lesson God brings out in Job 41:11*b* is that *everything* under heaven belongs to Him!

Some have suggested that leviathan is a picture of Satan. Compare Job 41:34*b* with Isaiah 14:12–17 and Revelation 12:9. What do you think?

One thing is for certain: God is greater than both leviathan (Job 41:10) and that great dragon, Satan (Revelation 14:9–12).

Memory Verse

Colossians 3:16*a*

"Let the word of Christ dwell in you richly in all wisdom."

Lesson Ten

Waiting on Our Great God

Opener

What's your initial reaction when someone tells you, "Just wait a minute"?

"Just wait." Those aren't exactly our favorite words, are they? What does it mean to wait? Is it staring into space, twirling your hair, and daydreaming your time away? Is it stewing over how rude so-and-so is to waste your time like this? Is it wishing you were just a few years older so that you could drive or date or something else?

We all have to wait at times—on friends, on family members, for test scores, for birthdays, for Christmas, and more. Waiting is a part of living in this world. But waiting on the Lord is more than just passing time.

Waiting on the Lord is a multifaceted gemstone in the treasure chest of Christianity. It involves expectation, patient endurance, service, solitude, and complete dependence. That sounds like a lot, but we'll break it down and look at each of those aspects as we go along in this lesson. And our purpose will be to find out what it means to wait on the Lord, what we are to be doing while we wait, and what our reaction should be when He gives us our portion.

Focus Passage

Read Psalm 104:27–28.

Finding Out God's Greatness

"These wait all upon thee" (Psalm 104:27). Each and every creature in God's universe waits for Him. Throughout Scripture God tells us to wait on Him. But what does that mean? What does it mean to wait on the Lord?

Perhaps it would help to look at what all these creatures wait on God for. What are they waiting for (Psalm 104:27)?

_____

Confident Expectation
In lesson three, we established that we are God's servants. Read Psalm 123:2. How do we look to the Lord?

_____

In Proverbs 31:15 the virtuous woman is rising early to prepare a portion of food for her family. She graciously thinks of those in her employ and sets aside a good portion for them as well. Her servants can *expect* to be taken care of as long as they're working for her.

In the same way, with God as our master, we can expect Him to give us each a good portion on a daily basis.

Patient Endurance
Patience in Scripture often carries the idea of enduring or persevering in the face of grief. Read James 5:7–11. Fill in the chart below with who waits, or waited, patiently according to these verses.

Verse	Who Waits Patiently
James 5:7	The husbandman or farmer
James 5:10	

Verse	Who Waits Patiently
James 5:11	

- Farmers have to persevere in the field, *waiting patiently* for the rains.

- The prophets often *endured* very difficult things as they proclaimed the Word of the Lord to people who didn't want to hear what they were saying.

- Job suffered incredibly, having to *endure* a bitter wife and friends who were falsely accusing him of sin, as He *waited* for the Lord to teach him the lessons He had for him.

According to James 5:8, who is also supposed to be patient?

_____

Until when (James 5:7)?

_____

And what are you **not** supposed to do towards those who cause you grief (James 5:9)?

_____

How is God referred to in James 5:9?

_____

Christ's return is coming. Our great God is also our Judge, and He will make all things right at that time. Until then, we are to endure grief and persevere with patience.

Enthusiastic Service

There seems to be a connection between waiting on the Lord and serving Him. Paul praised the Thessalonian believers for placing their hope—their confident expectation—in Christ's return, for *enduring* under affliction, and for *serving* Him in the meantime (1 Thessalonians 1:2–10).

Read Titus 2:11–14. What has God's grace taught us we should live like (Titus 2:12)?

1. _____

2. _____

3. _____

What are we to be looking for and waiting for in patient expectation (Titus 2:13)?

_____

What are we to be zealous or enthusiastic about in the meantime (Titus 2:14)?

_____

As we enthusiastically do good in our service for God and others, God knows our tendency is to become weary. In Galatians Paul encourages us to "not be weary in well doing: for in due season we shall reap, if we faint not" (Galatians 6:9).

Isaiah reminds us that God is never weary and He never becomes faint. Read Isaiah 40:28–31. How can we overcome weariness—fatigue, faintness, and a desire to quit?

_____

There's that phrase again: "Wait upon the Lord" (Isaiah 40:31)!

Strengthening Quiet Times

Look at Isaiah 40:28–31 one more time. Notice that as we wait on the Lord we are made like Him. He is strong, and as we wait on Him, we are made strong. I think this truth gives us a clue to what it means to wait on the Lord: it is as we spend time alone in the Word of God (Psalm 130:5; James 1:25) that we are changed to be like Him (2 Corinthians 3:18).

What are we to keep before the Lord in order to renew our strength according to Isaiah 41:1*a*?

_____

I think it's significant that in Isaiah 40:31 those that *"wait* upon the Lord" have the same result—renewed strength—as those who "keep *silence"* before Him in Isaiah 41:1.

In what do we find strength according to Isaiah 30:15?

_____

"In quietness and in confidence" seems to be just one more way of saying, "Wait on the Lord."

Complete Dependence

In the context of Job, Elihu was telling Job he must trust God's judgments and decisions and that he must wait patiently for the Lord to reveal His intentions to Job. Job 35:14 says "therefore trust thou in Him." Another translation (NASB) reads "you must wait for Him". "Trusting in the Lord" and "waiting on the Lord" are interchangeable at least to some extent, which makes sense because *waiting* on the LORD is accomplished by *trusting* in and *depending* on our great God!

Let's go back to Psalm 104:27–28 now that we have looked in some detail at what it means to wait upon the Lord. "These wait all upon thee" teaches us that each of God's creations must look to the Lord for their needs. They can *expect* Him to provide, and they are completely *dependent* on Him!

When does God provide (Psalm 104:27*b*)?

_____

And what does God expect us to do with what He provides (Psalm 104:28*a*)?

_____

Remember that God's hand is full of bountiful riches. When He takes what is in His hand and gives it to us, what should we realize (Psalm 104:28*b*)?

God asked Job if he would dare to nullify and overthrow God's judgments, His discernment, and His choices for Job's life. Would he attempt to say that God was wrong and he was right? (Job 40:8).

In the end, Job concluded that he knew that God was the only One Who knows and controls everything. Nothing—not even one thought—was unknown to Him, and God did not have to explain every "why?" to Job (Job 42:2–6).

James records that the over-arching lesson God had in mind for Job was that God is merciful and full of compassion (James 5:11). In other words, God is good! We must conclude the same thing!

You and I cannot begin to grasp God's wonderful plan (Romans 11:33). He alone knows everything and works each detail of our lives out for our good (Romans 8:28).

Our responsibility is to accept what He has given us and to respond in love and service for Him. That, after all, is what it means to wait on the Lord!

Reflections

Do you feel like you have a better understanding of what it means to wait on the Lord?

If someone were to ask you what it means to wait on the Lord, what would you tell them in one or two sentences?

Do you *expect* God to give you a good portion?

Are you patiently enduring whatever hard thing the Lord has allowed into your life right now?

_____

Are you looking for Christ's return with a joyful hope and confident expectation?

_____

What are you doing to serve the Lord and love others while you wait?

_____

Are you finding strength as you spend quiet time in God's Word on a consistent basis?

_____

Will you choose to trust in the Lord and depend completely on Him for all your needs and desires?

_____

What part of God's portion for you right now is hard to accept?

_____

Do you believe God's judgments or decisions to be best for you, or are you tempted to think you might know better sometimes?

_____

Will you choose to praise our great God for giving you the portion He has chosen to give you right now and acknowledge that His ways are "too wonderful" for you to completely understand (Psalm 139:6)?

_____

Additional Study

If you're baby-sitting and a two-year-old asks you for a snack, are you going to give him the whole bag of animal crackers? I hope not! Why?

I can think of at least three reasons (though I'm sure there could be more):

1. They'd end up all over the floor, and you'd have to pick them up.

2. If his mom found out you gave him the entire bag, she may not ask you to baby-sit for him ever again.

3. It's just not good for him!

You know better than a toddler. And just because he complains doesn't mean he gets his way. Similarly, God knows better than we do, even as young adults. He knows what's best for us, and if we're smart we won't complain about not getting what He knows isn't good for us.

Consider Psalm 106:15, Matthew 26:39, and Psalm 16:1–11.

Memory Verse

Psalm 62:5, 8

"My soul, wait thou only upon God; for my expectation is from him. . . . Trust in him at all times; ye people, pour out your heart before him: God is a refuge for us. Selah."

Lesson Eleven
Living in the Presence of Our Great God

Opener

I did it too as a teen, but it still always made me laugh as the receptionist at a Christian school when two, or even three, girls would come up to the office asking for *one* safety pin.

Guys sometimes make fun of how we girls all seem to go to the bathroom at the same time or how we go up to get a refill at a restaurant together. But it's moral support, and it makes us feel good. We like having a friend with us. Her mere presence somehow helps us feel more secure—morally supported, I guess.

In this next passage in Psalm 104, our psalmist draws our attention to the necessity of living in the awesome *presence* of our great God.

Focus Passage

Read Psalm 104:29–32.

Finding Out God's Greatness

What happens when God hides His face (Psalm 104:29)?

Though God is always near, sometimes it seems as if He's hiding. Several of the psalm writers experienced these times and expressed their emotions in song. Perhaps you too have gone through times when it seems God is silent or far away.

Read Psalm 22:1–24. Have you ever felt dejected and forsaken like David did?

_____

Christ felt the supreme agony of God's abandonment when He bore the penalty for our sins on the cruel cross at Calvary (Matthew 27:46). While Christ was suffering on the cross, what phrase did He quote from Psalm 22?

_____

What is the penalty or payment of sin (Romans 6:23a)?

_____

The death referred to in Romans 6:23 is literally a separation from God's presence. Christ bore that penalty—the agony of being separated from His Father—so that you and I could experience the joy of God's presence forever by simply accepting His gift to us of eternal life (Romans 6:23).

God is holy and cannot look on sin. When David realized the dreadfulness of his sin with Bathsheba and of killing her husband Uriah as part of his cover-up, perhaps his greatest fear was that God would shut him out of His presence and all the blessings that go along with it. What does David pray in Psalm 51:11?

_____

Each sin you commit is like a brick placed between you as a believer and your great God. With each additional sin, Satan gains another stronghold, smothers on the mortar, and laughs as the brick wall gets taller and taller.

Satan's greatest delight is to see you or me lose fellowship with God, to see a distancing come in our relationship with God, to see us separated from God's presence.

God's desire is that we would confess our sins and experience His forgiveness. His forgiveness is like a mighty flood that hits a brick wall, no matter how tall or wide that wall is, and destroys it in one swift torrent. It is only when we have confessed our sins and been forgiven that we can finally experience the joy of His presence (Psalm 16:11).

Without God's presence, we are left to our own troubled selves. According to Psalm 104:29b, what happens if He takes our breath away?

_____

Read Job 33:4 and Acts 17:24–25. Who gave us our breath in the first place?

_____

Read Genesis 2:7. What did God make man out of?

_____

And what did God's breathing into man's nostrils "the breath of life" make man become?

_____

As a living soul, man is accountable—responsible or answerable—to God for his choices. God told Adam and Eve not to eat of the tree of the knowledge of good and evil. According to Genesis 3:3, what would be the consequence of their choice to disobey?

_____

What would Adam return to (Genesis 3:19; Job 34:14–15)?

_____

Read James 4:14. What does James point out that we don't know?

_____

And what does he compare life to?

_____

James strongly states that life is short. We know that life will end (Hebrews 9:27), but we don't know when. Within a span of two years when I was in high school, three teens from either my Christian school or church youth group were killed in traffic accidents. To say the least, their deaths impacted my life as a teen. We like to think we have years ahead of us, but the truth is we can't really know.

It would do each of us well to be prepared for whenever God may choose to take away our breath. Read Hebrews 9:27. What comes after your appointment with death?

___

Let's go back to Psalm 104. God not only removes His presence or our breath, but He also does what according to verse 30?

___

The prophet Ezekiel saw some pretty amazing visions, as recorded in the book of Ezekiel. Chapters 36 and 37 of that book are perhaps the most awesome where God promises revival and renewal to the nation of Israel.

God's people had sinned, and He had sent them into captivity to bring them to repentance. Sin is disgusting to God. But the main theme of Ezekiel is that the nations would "know that" He is "the Lord" (Ezekiel 36:23). And so, for His own great name's sake, God decides to cleanse His people from their sins.

Read Ezekiel 37:1. Where did Ezekiel find himself in this vision?

___

What was the valley full of (Ezekiel 37:1)?

___

Read Ezekiel 37:2–4. How did Ezekiel answer the Lord's question, "Can these bones live?"

___

Read Ezekiel 37:5–10. What happened to the dry bones?

_____

Read Ezekiel 37:11–14. Do you see a connection between this passage and Psalm 104:30?

_____

We need revival and renewal today as much as the people of Israel in Ezekiel's day. They said, "Our bones are dried, and our hope is lost" (Ezekiel 37:11).

It is so easy to lose hope when we get our eyes off God and onto our circumstances. There are so many worldly attractions competing for our attentions and affections.

But if we will turn to God in humility, our hope can be found again. When your spirit is disquieted or troubled, determine with the writer of Psalms 42 and 43 to "hope thou in God: for I shall yet praise him, who is the health [or help] of my countenance, and my God" (Psalm 42:5, 11; 43:5).

Read Psalm 51:7–12. David longed for forgiveness and for renewed joy. Record verses 10 and 12 below.

Psalm 51:10

_____

_____

_____

Psalm 51:12

_____

_____

_____

As God revives us and renews His Spirit in us, we are then able to have a ministry for the Lord (Psalm 51:13) and to praise the Lord (Psalm 51:14–15)! God is so good to restore us again and again.

Let's go back again to Psalm 104. Read verse 31. What must "endure forever"?

_____

God's glory is His special presence.

In the Old Testament, this special presence of God was called the shekinah glory. It appeared in the cloud in the wilderness as well as in the tabernacle and the temple (Exodus 16:10; 40:34; Numbers 14:10; 1 Kings 8:10–11).

In the New Testament, God's special presence is His Spirit. Just as the shekinah glory filled the Old Testament temple, so the Spirit of God fills the New Testament believer (1 Corinthians 6:19; Ephesians 5:18). (*Scofield's Study Bible*, note on Exodus 40:34).

So in Psalm 104:29 the psalmist realized that when God's presence is withdrawn, he might as well die. But in Psalm 104:30 he rejoices in the blessing of God's presence in its reviving abilities. And in Psalm 104:31 he cries out in earnestness for God's special presence to endure forever. Is that your heart's greatest desire too—for God's presence to *always* be present in your life?

_____

Again, what do we find in God's presence according to Psalm 16:11?

_____

God delights in giving us joy and godly pleasures because He is our great God!

Read Psalm 104:32. Have you ever heard another girl say, "He looked at me!" in an awe-stricken voice? Most of the time that's pretty pathetic, but for some reason certain guys have that heart-melting effect on certain girls.

Imagine, though, what it would be like to have the God of all creation look at you! "He looketh on the earth, and it trembleth: he toucheth the hills, and they smoke" (Psalm 104:32). Do you respond to the Lord's presence with awe and respectful amazement?

How does the author of Hebrews describe our God in Hebrews 12:29?

If we would remember that God's name is El Roi: Thou God Seest Me (Genesis 16:13) and realize that "the eyes of the Lord are in every place" (Proverbs 15:3), perhaps we would live a little differently.

According to Ezekiel 36:27, what does God cause and expect us to do when we have His Spirit?

Awesome seems to be one of those overused words in our society. The word *awesome* literally means worthy of awe. That's an easy enough breakdown even without pulling out a dictionary. But do you and I understand the true awesomeness of our great God? Do you realize His presence is with you? Do you live in the reality that God sees you all the time? Do you consciously realize that His Holy Spirit, His special presence, lives inside of you? Take a few moments right now to reflect on these realities.

Finally, Psalm 104:31b says, "The Lord shall rejoice in his works." God loves what He's created!

Read Revelation 4:11. What is the purpose of God's creation?

As God looks down at the earth and sees you and me, we should desire that He would be able to rejoice in us as we seek to know and obey Him. We desperately need to think about Him, to live in the reality of His presence minute by minute, and to find all our joy and pleasure—our satisfaction—in Him!

Reflections

Have you experienced the pain of God's silence? Or has He seemed to be far away? Have you experienced the awfulness of having some sin separating you from the Lord?

_____

Is there some sin that you need to confess to the Lord right now and ask for forgiveness and restored fellowship? Pause and take some time to do so right now if there is.

_____

Who gave you breath? And Who decides how long your life will be? Do you trust Him with your life and breath?

_____

Are you living your life in such a way that it is obvious that you desire God's special presence to be with you forever?

_____

Is your life bringing pleasure to God?

_____

Additional Study

Read Romans 8:1–6, Galatians 5:16–26; Ephesians 2:1–10 and meditate on the difference between living in the flesh versus living in the Spirit.

Verses	In the flesh	In the spirit
Romans 8:1–6	•	•
	•	•
	•	•
	•	•

Verses	In the flesh	In the spirit
Galatians 5:16–26	◆ ◆	◆ ◆ ◆ ◆
Ephesians 2:1–10	◆ ◆	◆ ◆

Memory Verse

Ezekiel 36:27–29*a*

"And I will put my spirit within you, and cause you to walk in my statutes, and ye shall keep my judgments, and do them. . . . and ye shall be my people, and I will be your God. I will also save you from all your uncleannesses."

Lesson Twelve
Worshiping Our Great God

Opener

Do you know any brothers or sisters who are complete opposites? They have the same parents, but that's about the only thing they have in common?

There was a set of brothers like this in Bible. Their names were Cain and Abel. And they had two very different ways of doing things.

Cain was older with every firstborn tendency imaginable. No one would tell *him* what to do. He was a "tiller of the ground," the Bible says (Genesis 4:2). I imagine he was pretty good at it too, producing only the finest vegetation outside the garden of Eden. But he had a weakness—pride. He thought he knew better . . . even than God.

Abel, perhaps growing up in the shadow of his older brother, learned to be humble. He was a "keeper of sheep" (Genesis 4:2).

Both Cain's and Abel's occupations were appropriate means of providing for a family, a balanced diet being made up of a combination of their products.

Since Cain and Abel's parents, Adam and Eve, had disobeyed God, it was necessary to offer sacrifices in order to maintain a right relationship with God. God had instituted the sacrificial system because He wanted to have fellowship with mankind. The blood of a lamb being sacrificed was God's plan to cover sin until His Son, Jesus Christ, would come and die to take away the sin of the world (John 1:29).

There is no doubt in my mind that Adam and Eve taught their boys the proper way to worship God. Abel brought the best of his flock, as God had required. Cain, on the other hand, thought he knew better. He decided he would offer produce from his own works—fruits and vegetables.

In Genesis 4:4–5 we find that "the Lord had respect unto Abel and to his offering: but unto Cain and to his offering he had not respect."

In today's lesson, we will learn about true worship—what God accepts and deserves. In the end, we will see that our great God deserves true worship from all of His creation, which especially includes you and me.

Focus Passage

I think it's important as we come to the conclusion of our study to make sure that we have the big picture of Psalm 104 in mind. Go back and read it one more time. Our focus passage will be Psalm 104:33–35.

Finding Out God's Greatness

True worship—worship that God accepts—involves songs of praise, sweet meditation, steadfast joyfulness, and sin being either confessed or consumed. We'll consider each of these aspects of worship as we take a closer look into the last three verses of this psalm.

Songs of Praise

What two things does the psalmist say he *will* do in verse 33?

1. _____

_____

2. _____

_____

How long will he sing (verse 33)?

_____

"As long as I live" covers the scope of this life—from now until I die. But he doesn't stop there; he goes on to say, "while I have my being," which extends from this life through all of eternity!

If you are saved, you will be praising God forever in heaven. But we also need to resolve to praise Him by singing while we are still here on earth.

Most of us have made resolutions: "I will or will not _(fill in the blank)_" for "_(fill in amount of time)_." I remember when I was a junior in high school I resolved to not drink any soda pop for an entire year. I know, you're thinking I was crazy, and maybe you're right, but regardless, it was a resolution. I was involved in volleyball and track, and neither coach wanted us to drink pop. So I decided if it wasn't good for game days, maybe it would be good if I didn't drink it at all. It was important to me to be in good shape, so I kept my resolve. Other resolutions, however, have fallen by the wayside at times, even resolutions that should have been more important to me than whether I drank pop or not—like daily devotions or contentment. God has to work those things in us— "both to will" or to really want to and then to actually "do of his good pleasure" (Philippians 2:13).

Throughout Psalms, we see recorded how God had worked a desire in each psalmists' heart to sing praise to Him. Read Psalm 108:1–3. Look at how David begins that psalm: "O God, my heart is fixed." I am resolved. I am determined. I am steadfast. I have made up my mind. I am dead set on this!

How many times does David say "I will" in those three verses (Psalm 108:1–3)?

_____

And what are his resolutions?

_____

I've heard it said that more lies are told while holding a hymnal than at any other time. That could very well be true. Have you ever caught yourself singing along with some familiar song and realized that you had no clue what you just sang? It happens all too easily, especially for those of us who have regular chapel times at school or family devotions. Let me challenge you to think about the words of songs as you sing and make sure that you believe what you are singing.

God deserves worship that is sincere and honest. Read Matthew 15:7–9. What did Christ call those who said the "right" things but didn't have a right heart (Matthew 15:7)?

_____

Though they drew near with what they said, where were their hearts (Matthew 15:8)?

_____

What did Christ say their worship was (Matthew 15:9a)?

_____

Something that is vain is empty, literally *worthless* or *good for nothing*. Instead of being vain, we should want our worship to be real and profitable, giving God the full worth and honor He deserves.

You may be wondering, *so what is right worship*? Jesus Christ Himself gives us the answer in John 4:23–24 in His discussion with the Samaritan woman at the well. How must we worship God?

1. _____

2. _____

Worship that is *not* consistent with the truths of God's Word is not pleasing to God, *even if* the worshiper has a great attitude and a sincere heart. Similarly, worship that *is* consistent with the truths of God's

Word but is done by someone who does *not* have the right heart attitude toward God is also not pleasing to our great God. True worship must be done "in spirit," that means with the right attitude, *and* "in truth," which means in the right way if it is to bring glory and pleasure to our great God.

Coming back to Psalm 104, worshiping God "in spirit and in truth" includes when we sing. We need to know that we're singing words and music that are consistent with His truth and that we are singing with the right heart attitude or spirit.

God deserves our worship. He is the Creator God. He is our King. He is our Redeemer. We have so much to praise Him for, yet too often we are more concerned that someone else might hear us, so we whisper our songs. I do not believe that our psalmist in Psalm 104 whispered his songs. And though it's not wrong to sing quietly, it is important that we sing with all our hearts and not be afraid to lift our voices.

Sweet Meditation

Scriptural meditation is simply thinking about God and His Word and how they apply to your life.

What does Psalm 104:34 say that this kind of Scriptural meditation will be?

Perhaps you've been at a basketball game and seen a "sweet" shot. It leaves you with a "Wow!" factor. This is the kind of amazement that we should have as we think on and see the sweet words and works of God.

As you meditate on God and His Word, that meditation will become more and more sweet to you. And it will be sweet to God as He hears your innermost thoughts (Psalm 139:14).

Steadfast Joyfulness

In Psalm 104:34b our psalmist declares one more "I will." What is it?

In 1 Kings 8, Solomon held a magnificent worship service to dedicate the temple. It would be similar to a dedication service your church might have when you build a new building. There was preaching, prayer, and praise. And the result was that the people went home "joyful and glad of heart." Read 1 Kings 8:66. Why were the people so happy?

The same can be true for you. As you see the greatness of our God, Who He is, and what He has done for you, you too will be able to rejoice.

In Deuteronomy 28:47, God rebuked His people because they did *not* obey the Lord and serve Him with joyfulness and gladness of heart. They could have received blessings if they had simply chosen to obey happily, but instead they were cursed. Obedience—both the act and the attitude—is always a choice. And every choice has consequences.

Sin—Confessed or Consumed

Look back to Psalm 104:35. We have all this praise, praise, praise, and then—BOOM! "Let the sinners be consumed out of the earth, and let the wicked be no more." How does that fit?

The first several times I read this passage, it seemed like some injunction thrown in out of nowhere. So I pulled out some commentaries and started researching, and it finally clicked: true worship is pure and holy worship.

This whole section has been talking about true worship. And sin cannot be a part of that worship because sin is *im*pure and *un*holy!

Read Psalm 29:2 and 96:9. How are we to worship the Lord?

Most of us would admit that we like looking pretty. We want to be beautiful. And yet it's important to understand what real beauty is. As you walk through a mall or department store, you will see popular fashions modeled on the manikins. Those styles may be considered *appealing* to the modern world of fashion design, but too often they are *appalling* to the designer of beauty—our great God.

In Psalm 29:2 and 96:9, God tells us what He thinks is beautiful: holiness. *Holiness* means unique excellence or set-apartness. As a Christian, God has set you apart for something uniquely excellent, something very special—intimate fellowship with Him.

Think about it this way: Do you have anything that is set aside only for special occasions? You protect that thing from everyday use. You don't want anything to ruin it. It is not for just anyone to enjoy. No, it is reserved for your special purposes. For example, your mom would probably not be too happy if she came home to find your brother and his friends using her grandmother's china for their football party, and you would not be too pleased to find your kid sister playing dress up in your closet.

That is the way Christ sees you, only even more so. God calls Himself our Husband (Isaiah 54:5). Read Ephesians 5:22–33. You, as part of the Church, are Christ's chosen bride, His wife. A husband expects his wife to be completely set apart for his own enjoyment. And God expects no less. What does Christ want to present Himself (Ephesians 5:27)?

_____

What did Christ do that this might be possible (Ephesians 5:25)?

_____

And what does He use to purify us (Ephesians 5:26)?

_____

I don't know how many times we've come back to this in our study. The Word of God is central to the Christian life! As you read the Word of God and apply it to your life, God will make you holy. He will make you *beautiful*! And in that state of beautiful holiness, you will be able to truly worship the Lord!

In addition to His Word, sometimes God uses trials to perfect and purify us. Read 1 Peter 1:7. Gold is passed through fire to be purified—to separate out any alloy, anything less than the pure gold. When God uses trials to purify us, how do we come out in comparison with gold?

_____

Job said, "He knoweth the way that I take: when he hath tried me, I shall come forth as gold" (Job 23:10). We must have this confidence that God is making us pure, holy, and beautiful, even if, like Job, we don't always understand the fiery process.

Still other times God uses chastening or punishment to purify us. Read Hebrews 12:6–11. Whom does the Lord chasten (verse 6)?

_____

Our parents disciplined us as kids as they saw fit "after their own pleasure" (Hebrews 12:10). Why does God chasten us, according to that same verse?

_____

Holiness is not just something that God is doing *to* us. We have a responsibility to keep ourselves pure also, making right choices. Read 1 Peter 1:14–17. What are we to be as (verse 14)?

_____

Is 1 Peter 1:15–16 given as an option or as a command?

_____

Why are we to be holy (1 Peter 1:16)?

_____

What is God going to do "without respect of persons" (without showing any favoritism, no matter who you are) according to 1 Peter 1:17?

_____

As we go back to Psalm 104:34, we realize this isn't just the psalmist wishing for God to consume the wicked; it's a statement of fact. God is going to judge the world, and whatever is corrupting the beauty of His holy and wonderful works will have to be eliminated.

On a personal level, as God reveals sin in your life and in mine, we must confess our sins and call sin, sin—not a disease or a disorder or just a mistake. We must repent of and turn away from that sin and claim God's promised forgiveness (1 John 1:9). And we must pursue holiness so that we can properly worship God (Hebrews 12:14).

What does Psalm 97:10 reveal to be true about those who love God?

_____

Conclusion

Going back one last time to Psalm 104, we have come to the beautiful conclusion of this song of praise. What portion of verse 35 is repeated from verse 1?

_____

So the psalmist ends where he began, only now with even greater enthusiasm than before. He is even more convinced of the greatness of our God. He has seen Who God is and the manifold works He has done. He has learned that God is in control of every facet of life, that He will satisfy him, and that His presence is what gives him life. He has begun worshiping the Lord in the beauty of holiness. He will continue singing praises to his God and enjoying the sweetness of meditating on Him. He is resolved to praise the Lord. He can do nothing else. His soul is full of the goodness of the Lord. He is overflowing with joy in our great God.

And now He invites you and me to join Him singing "Hallelujah!" or literally, "Praise ye the Lord!"

As you and I continue "finding out God's greatness" and as we find satisfaction in worshiping Him the right way—with songs of praise, sweet meditation, steadfast joyfulness, and sins repented of and for-given—we too will desire others to come and join us in praising our great God!

Reflections

Will you resolve to worship God in what and how you sing?

Will you resolve to sing to God and not be so concerned with what those around you think about your vocal abilities?

Do you worship the Lord "in spirit" with a sincere heart of love "and in truth," determining to be consistent with the Word of God and not stray from it? Do you struggle more with one than the other?

Is your meditation or what you think about sweet to God?

Do you find meditating on God, Who He is and what He's done, to be sweet?

Will you resolve to be glad in the Lord, to rejoice in Him no matter what?

Will you resolve to be holy and beautiful for God rather than trying to attract attention from guys in a worldly way?

Will you resolve to the love the Lord and hate evil (Psalm 97:10)? Is there any sin in your life that you need to confess?

Are you spending time in His Word so that He can cleanse you that way?

Is there some hard thing in your life that God may be using to purify you? Are you willing to go through trials or chastening if it means you will come out pure and beautiful to God?

After completing this study and "finding out God's greatness," are you excited with the psalmist to praise the Lord?

Do you want others to see our great God and praise Him with you?

Additional Study

Psalms 96–98 praise the Lord for His judgment. Sometimes we like to praise God for His goodness and love and just accept, but not praise Him for, His judgment. But we *can* actually praise Him for being a God of justice because that means He will make everything right in the end.

Memory Verse

Psalm 97:10, 12

"Ye that love the Lord, hate evil. . . . Rejoice in the Lord, ye righteous; and give thanks at the remembrance of his holiness."

Finding Out God's Greatness

A Continuing Goal

Congratulations! You have completed all twelve lessons in *No Matter What*! But what's even more exciting is that you've only just begun discovering the greatness of our God.

I would recommend that you continue getting to know your great God by journeying through the book of Psalms and looking for Who God is and what your response should be to Him.

Another idea might be going through Psalms and making a list of "I Know My God Is Great Because . . ." You can read a psalm a day and finish the book in about five months, or you could read five psalms a day and complete the whole book of Psalms in just one month. You may just want to read Psalms on Saturday or Sunday and do other reading throughout the week. These are just some ideas.

Because of the discoveries you've already made in Psalm 104, I think whichever approach you take, you will find your eyes opened to new treasures throughout the Psalms.

Our psalmist seems to have surrounded himself with nature as he meditated on God and His wonderful works. Whenever you have the opportunity to be out in nature for your devotional time, let me urge you to take advantage of it. There is something very special about sitting by the lake at summer camp or even on the patio in your own backyard during the warmer months of the year. So put forth the extra effort and get out there. And whether you have your Bible with you or not, whenever you are out in the middle of creation, "remember now thy Creator in the days of thy youth" (Ecclesiastes 12:1).

May God bless you as you continue finding out His greatness, and as you choose to rejoice . . . no matter what.

Discovering Treasure in Our Great God's Word
Study Helps for Personal Devotions

Tools to Help You Dig for Treasure

These are resources that will help you understand what you are reading and connect it with other passages in Scripture.

Commentary

A commentary is a book that contains another person's detailed notes on a book or books of the Bible. Often, these books go verse by verse and can be used as a reference to gain insight on specific phrases or even words in a verse. My top pick for Psalms is Charles Spurgeon's *Treasury of David*.

Concordance

Many Bibles have a simple concordance in the back. Concordances give a list of verses that contain a specific key word. Use this to do word studies or to find a verse that you may remember a part of but not the whole thing. The most thorough concordance (which includes all occurrences of whatever word you're studying in the King James Version) is *Strong's Concordance*. You can also find concordances online for other versions.

Cross-Reference

Many times as you're reading a passage you'll see a little letter super-scripted next to a word or phrase. That directs you to either a center or side column with references to verses in other places in the Bible that would be somehow connected to the verse you are studying.

Dictionary

Using a regular dictionary is a helpful way to make sure you understand what the words of Scripture mean. There are also Bible dictionaries that can give you a little more detailed definition of what that word would have meant in Bible times.

Thesaurus

Using a thesaurus, like a dictionary, can be helpful in giving a fuller understanding of the word. A thesaurus won't give a definition but will give you synonyms for the word you're studying.

Translation

Looking up the word in another translation of Scripture may also be a tool to discover synonyms or to get a fuller grasp on what a particular verse or phrase means.

The Right Approach to Digging

This is not so much what you do during your daily devotional time but with what attitude you do it—how you approach God's Word. The following heart attitudes will help you get a more accurate picture of yourself as you study the Scriptures and search for treasure.

Respect

Maintain the highest respect for God's Word. It is unlike any other book. It is alive and powerful (Hebrews 4:12). Christ is referred to as the Word made flesh (John 1:1, 14).

Honesty

Be willing to admit your struggles. Be totally honest with yourself and before the Lord. He already knows everything anyway. We can't hide from Him. Truly, in studying the Bible as in all of life, honesty is the best policy.

Willingness to Change

Having a heart that is willing to make changes is the only way to spiritual success. You can't kick against the pricks and expect to grow from them at the same time. Accept what God is doing in your life. Be willing for Him to work on you.

Determination

This is a must if you are to tackle a project. You will come to bumps in the road, hills, and sometimes even foreboding mountains. But be determined to dig and climb and tackle the task. It will be worth it in the end. Know that all along the way, God is with you and wants you to learn and grow in the knowledge and understanding of Him.

Techniques to Help You Understand What You've Found

It is a terrible misfortune for you and me to have treasures lying right before us in our Bibles and to not see them for what they really are. This section deals with proper interpretation as you look at a passage.

Context

Make sure you take verses in context, not trying to make them say what you'd like them to say but taking them for what they were intended to say. This may mean backing up and reading a few more verses or even a chapter or two, but the time invested will be worth it.

Literal Interpretation

Take what the Bible says at face value. Don't try to spiritualize straightforward truths. This will make your Bible study much easier and more enjoyable as well as more accurate and profitable.

Techniques for Using the Treasure You've Found

These are ways you can personalize and apply the treasures you've found to your life. Doing so will help you to be changed into a beautiful gem for God from the inside out forever.

Questioning

This is a strategy to help you learn how to begin meditating. As you study through a passage, get the details down. Find out the facts of what's going on—the old "Who, What, Where, When, How" list is helpful. Then as you're ready for digging deeper, ask the "Why" question.

Personalization

Take time to reflect. Whenever you read your Bible, personalize it. Ask God to show you how what you are reading applies to your life.

Prayer

Prayer is vital to studying the Bible. It is the Spirit Who gives enlightenment, shines the light on truth, and makes it real to you.

Accountability

Perhaps the greatest help to you as you work on mastering Scripture will be an accountability partner. This can be a friend, a parent, a teacher, or another person you respect. Knowing someone is going to be checking on you can really help you stay committed to changing a habit or conquering a temptation.

Treasuring What You've Found

Here are a few methods for treasuring God's Word in your heart (Psalm 119:11).

Meditation

Throughout your day, think on the things you've been studying. Just stop and take the time to chew on them and how those truths practically apply to you.

Memorization

Scripture memory is a key to winning the spiritual battle. Those verses are your weapons against Satan.

Journaling

Whether it's recording answers or copying out a verse, there's something about writing that gets information into our brains more concretely than if we just read it or hear it. Even though it takes extra time, it's well worth the effort.

Singing

As you begin or end your devotional time, use a hymnal. Try to learn hymns that you can sing to the Lord. Most hymnals are organized into groups—praise and worship, confession, the Christian warfare, and so on. I personally enjoy using a hymnal that has an index of Scripture references that go along with the songs.

For example, a song that you might learn with this study of Psalm 104 is "Jesus, I Am Resting, Resting." Part of the first verse reads, "I am finding out the greatness of Thy loving heart."

Review

It's always good to review what you've studied in the past. Keep this study guide and any other spiritual journals together in a special place where you can get to them easily and review them from time to time. You'll be amazed at the process of growth God has brought you through.

Action

Take action on what you see. Make an effort to change any blemishes in your reflection by the grace of God. Be a "doer" of the Word (James 1:23, 25).

Is Our Great God Your God?

Discovering a Personal Relationship with God

Before someone realizes Who our great God really is, his or her universe is pretty small. In fact, most of the time, if you and I are honest, that "universe" revolves around one person—myself!

Isaiah was a man with talents and gifts. Related to royalty, he probably held a decent place in the palace. He was most likely well liked and had a pretty good opinion of himself . . . until one day when God gave him a vision of something bigger than himself. In Isaiah 6, after his beloved king Uzziah died, God revealed His throne room to Isaiah. And Isaiah's little universe crumbled.

Isaiah fell to the ground, overwhelmed with the reality of Who God is and who, in turn, he really was: "Woe is me! for I am undone; because I am a man of unclean lips, and I dwell in the midst of a people of unclean lips: for mine eyes have seen the King, the Lord of hosts" (Isaiah 6:5).

Isaiah acknowledged his own sinfulness and the holiness of God. At that point God cleansed Isaiah from his sin. Only then was Isaiah able to be used by God. His life was changed forever! Isaiah lost some of the respect and prestige he had once known, but he gained a right relationship with God and power in the presence of God.

Isaiah spent the rest of his life proclaiming the message "Behold your God!" (Isaiah 40:9).

Have you personally come to the place where *your* universe has come crashing down because you really saw God and His greatness? Have you been cleansed from your sins?

Do you have a right relationship with Him?

God says that we have all sinned. We have done wrong. And He has seen it (Isaiah 53:6; Romans 3:23; Proverbs 15:3)!

Sin always has a price—and it's always more expensive than it's worth! The first part of Romans 6:23 tells us that the price tag of your sin and mine is death, literally eternal separation from God.

But it doesn't stop there. The rest of Romans 6:23 exclaims, "but the gift of God is eternal life through Jesus Christ our Lord"!

You see, Jesus, the sinless Son of God, came to earth, lived, and died to pay the price for each one of your sins and my sins. "He was wounded for our transgressions, he was bruised for our iniquities: the chastisement of our peace was upon him; and with his stripes we are healed" (Isaiah 53:5). He then rose again, conquering sin and death forever.

Isaiah communicated the heart of our great God: "Wash you, make you clean; put away the evil of your doings from before mine eyes; cease to do evil; learn to do well. . . . Come now, and let us reason together, saith the Lord: though your sins be as scarlet, they shall be as white as snow; though they be red like crimson, they shall be as wool" (Isaiah 1:16–18).

The only way we can be clean in our hearts is through Jesus. Each of us must repent. You must turn from your sin and to the Lord. "I tell you," unless "ye repent, ye shall . . . perish" (Luke 13:3).

But God promises, "If we confess our sins, he is faithful and just to forgive us our sins, and to cleanse us from all unrighteousness" (1 John 1:9).

But my sin is too awful, you might argue. No, friend. Look at the list in 1 Corinthians 6:9–10. Verse 11 goes on to say, "And such were some of you: but ye are washed, but ye are sanctified, but ye are justified in the name of the Lord Jesus, and by the Spirit of our God."

Please, dear friend, repent and be saved. "Believe on the Lord Jesus Christ, and thou shalt be saved" (Acts 16:31). God will forgive you no matter who you are or what you have done. He promised He would, and He's already paid the price.

Accept your God as Savior of your soul! And then just keep looking to Him. As you do, know that He will teach you how to do what is right. "He will teach us of his ways, and we will walk in his paths" (Isaiah 2:3). Pour out your heart to Him in prayer, acknowledging His greatness and your great need of Him throughout each day (Psalm 62:8). Continue reading His Word, discovering more and more about Him, and growing closer and closer to Him (James 1:22–25; 2 Peter 3:18). And then serve Him with all your heart (1 Samuel 12:24; Isaiah 6:8).

Young lady, "come ye, and let us walk in the light of the Lord" (Isaiah 2:5). And then get excited, because the path you are now on—God's path of salvation and sanctification—just keeps getting better and better. "The path of the just is as the shining light, that shineth more and more unto the perfect day" (Proverbs 4:18).

Bibliography

Barnes, Albert. *Notes on the Old Testament: Psalms.* (Grand Rapids: Baker House, 1983).

Calvin, John. *Calvin's Commentaries*, vol. VI, *Psalms 93–150*, trans. James Anderson. (Grand Rapids: Baker Book House Co, 1984).

Dickson, David. *A Commentary on the Psalms: Two Volumes in One.* (Carlisle, PA: Banner of Truth Trust, 1995).

Henry, Matthew. *Matthew Henry's Commentary on the Whole Bible: Complete and Unabridged in One Volume.* (Peabody, MA: Hendrickson Publishers, 1991).

Keil, C. F. and F. Delitzsch. *Commentary on the Old Testament in Ten Volumes*, vol. V, *Psalms*, trans. James Martin. (Grand Rapids: William B. Eerdmans Publishing Co. 1975).

Scofield, C. I. ed. *The Scofield Study Bible*, KJV, (New York: Oxford, 1996, orig. pub. 1909).

Spurgeon, Charles. *The Treasury of David*, vol. V, *Psalm CIV to CXVIII.* (London: Marshall Brothers, Limited, 1878).

Strong, James. *Strong's Exhaustive Concordance of the Bible.* (Peabody, MA Hendrickson Publishers, no date).